The Path of Unconditional Love

THROUGH THE

EYE

OF A NEEDLE

Clement DeWall

Also by Clement DeWall

The Last Pope
The Diary of John Peter

Traditional Marriage
From Abraham to the Present

False Questions
Jesus. and Our Spiritual Path

Forgive 70X7
Our Forgotten Power

The Last Supper
Its First Century Development

To my wife,

Eileen Mackin,

For her encouragement and support

THROUGH THE

EYE

OF A NEEDLE

THE PATH OF

UNCONDITIONAL LOVE

Clement DeWall

Scripture Quotations

Quotations from the Holy Bible are from one of the following and designated by the associated abbreviation:

OEB: The Open English Bible

NHEB: The New Heart English Bible

To make biblical passages more readable, some verses have been reformatted into separate paragraphs; verse numbers have also been omitted.

CONTENTS

Preface

One of the most influential Christians of the second century was a man unknown to most Christians today: Marcion, a wealthy ship owner who lived from around the year 100 to about 160 CE.

Marcion established churches in Italy, Africa, Syria, and what is now Turkey. Some of these lasted until late in the fourth century — remarkable, since Marcion rejected marriage and demanded celibacy of all members, so that membership depended entirely on conversions.

His primary influence, however, is not attributed to his imitation of the apostle Paul in founding churches, but to his creation of the first canon or list of accepted, authoritative writings. Until Marcion's time, Christians supported their teachings mostly on the Septuagint version of the Jewish Scriptures. After he published his canon, other Christian groups fought back by developing their own canons.

Marcion rejected all the writings we include in the Old Testament today and listed only these: the Gospel according to Luke, which did not yet have a title; and these letters of Paul in this order: Galatians, Corinthians (First and Second combined), Romans, Thessalonians (First and Second combined), Laodiceans (now called Ephesians), Colossians, and Philemon. Other writings included in our New Testament, such as Hebrews and the Pastoral Epistles (First and Second Timothy and Titus), he omitted; it is possible that these writings were created after his time. When the Catholic canon was formed some centuries later, Romans was placed before the other Pauline epistles, probably to give the church in Rome the place of honor.

We do not have any of the original books in Marcion's canon. Instead, we rely on Tertullian (c. 155-240 CE) to tell us how they differed from what is in our New Testament. He relates that the Gospel of Luke, along with Galatians and Romans, are missing significant portions. While the majority of Scripture scholars believe that Marcion expunged these passages because of his beliefs, a significant number of others disagree. We know for certain that over time a number of passages were added to the original New Testament books, such as the various conclusions to Mark and the story of the woman caught in adultery in John 8. It has never been proved that Marcion changed or deleted anything in the books he held sacred, and there is no evidence that he changed any books except for Luke, Galatians, and Romans. Claims that he modified these are based on authors like Irenaeus and Tertullian, who were his theological adversaries.

Marcion wanted to get back to the original teachings of Jesus. Already in the second century Christian communities were condemning each other for their false beliefs. Irenaeus, bishop of Lyons, in his five-volume work, *Adversus Haereses (Against Heresies),* described over a dozen heretical beliefs. *Heresy,* in Greek meaning *choice,* included any doctrine with which Irenaeus disagreed. In Chapter XXVII of Book V, he described how heretics would be condemned at the time of judgment. "Love your enemies" did not apply to those Christian churches branded as heretical.

Marcion was reacting to the widespread emphasis on doctrines about Jesus in Christian churches when he decided to return to what Jesus taught. He recognized that Jesus had repeatedly taught lessons of forgiveness, love, and mercy to be initiated in our lives in imitation of God's love for us. But he faced the problem of reconciling Jesus's image of God with the many images of an angry, vengeful God in the Old Testament. He concluded that the Creator God of the Hebrews was not the same God as the Father proclaimed by Jesus. This doctrine of two gods, along with the rejection of all Jewish and Hebrew traditions and scriptures, determined that his theology would last but a few centuries.

Although Marcion failed to revive Jesus's teachings as the focal point of Christian doctrine, the need to do so today is more and more pressing. All Christian churches claim to preach the gospel, but they are divided by creeds and doctrines not found anywhere in the gospel they preach. Christianity seems to have lost its way, and we need to return to the spiritual path that Jesus taught and commanded.

My purpose here is to make Jesus's words the central message in order to fulfill our spiritual purpose of growing in love of God and neighbor. To do so can be a viable stepping stone to heal the wounds of division among Christian churches and to overcome the overwhelming conflicts over race, gender, politics, and social issues of today.

Introduction

On June 26, 1959, I was returning to the United States after four years of study in Rome. While at a brief layover in Milan, I was called to the ticket desk and informed that I had been scheduled to take TWA flight 891 to London. I sat down for a brief moment, and then for a reason I cannot explain, I returned to the agent and asked for another flight. She readily obliged, and I left for London on Alitalia.

On arriving in London, the family that was to meet me expressed both joy and shock when I walked through the door. I learned that the TWA plane was struck by lightning shortly after takeoff. There were no survivors.

I do not know why I made a decision that made the difference between immediate death and life for many more decades. Was it luck? Chance? My guardian angel? My choice can have multiple interpretations.

My decision is an example of every significant event. We observe what happens, and then we interpret or give the event a meaning — at least what the event means to us. I call this process perception or *perceiving,* a two-step mental process of observing and interpreting.

People can perceive the same event or fact in many ways. One reason for this is that we can *see* things differently; witnesses of the same crime can give contradictory testimony. But another overlooked reason is that they interpret an event or fact in diverse ways, depending on what is important or meaningful to them. A new drug may be seen as hopeful for someone with an incurable illness. To a pharmaceutical company it may be viewed as a valuable money maker. A politician may consider it a means to obtain campaign contributions, depending on the legislation to be passed. It is the same drug, viewed according to one's personal values. People can see the same fact or event and give it their own personal meaning.

Most day-to-day happenings are not sufficiently significant to discuss their interpretation. It is rarely of much concern at what time one gets out of bed in the morning or what one eats for breakfast. But the more facts or events increase in importance, the more we tend to interpret them and give them a specific meaning. And the meaning or interpretation we give is often of our own choice. If I offer an explanation of why I chose to fly Alitalia instead of TWA out of Milan in 1959, I cannot prove the reason for my decision. If I believe it was pure chance or if I think it was divine intervention, I do so because I freely choose that interpretation.

This book is about how to walk the path toward unconditional love of God and neighbor. The directions down this path come primarily from Jesus's message as preached in the Gospels of Matthew, Mark and Luke. The first step on this path is to *learn* and *practice* the way Jesus taught us to *perceive* reality. As we observe the world, we give it meaning according to his teachings. All the other practices proposed in this book depend on the fundamental practice of *perceiving* as Jesus taught us.

Our subject matter is dependent on what Jesus taught us about how to live and how to love — principles he made applicable to everyone without concern for culture or creed.

My approach in organizing the teachings of the Gospels into specific groupings cannot lay claim to being the only or best approach. Others may be equally suitable. However, this is the logic I have tried to follow: The first spiritual practice of *perceiving* lays out who you are and what your relationship with God and your fellow human beings is. The next two practices of *forgiving* and *blessing* deal with the attitude Jesus requires in reacting with others. The fourth practice of *giving thanks* describes the fundamental sense of appreciation necessary in our relationship with God and others. The fifth practice, *praying*, can come from one's routine, but should arise spontaneously from the previous practices. Toward the end of the book it will be noted that prayer, when offered routinely or in other circumstances, can also be an obstacle to love. The final practice takes up *showing unconditional love by acting*. The book concludes by pointing out missteps to avoid on one's spiritual path. These missteps are called *illusions,* because they lead to a misinterpretation of reality as Jesus preached it.

There are a number of topics that I do *not* cover: You will find nothing here about holiness or sanctity. These concepts imply that in some way God comes into us or changes us into something more sacred than other people. The words expressing holiness and sanctity are present throughout the Bible, but Jesus never told us how to become holy — only how to live.

Neither will you be told where to go searching for a spiritual teacher. Jesus frequently told those he had helped, "Your faith has saved you." It is *your* faith. He did not attribute being saved even to his own power.

Furthermore, it was the petitioners' *faith* that saved them. In the first century the Greek word for faith, *pistis,* meant faithfulness or steadfastness. In the second century it came to mean a set of beliefs or doctrines, but this denotation (or connotation) was foreign to the language of Jesus, who never gave us a creed or set of doctrines.

Jesus expected us to walk our spiritual path, from beginning to end, from *within us.* He offered no gurus to direct us. He failed to tell the Galileans they had to heed and obey his apostles or any other intermediaries. His directives were simple, aimed at common people.

We search the Gospels in vain for any secret techniques. Jesus taught no mantras, no breathing procedure, no practices of meditation, no requirement for a spiritual director. These may be beneficial, but they are not found in the Jesus's teachings.

Lacking, too, are any unique characteristics of sanctity, such as levitation, bilocation, ability to work miracles, or precognition, as well as special phases one has to pass through, such as the dark night of the soul, described by Theresa of Avila and John of the Cross.

Since I adhere as strictly as possible to using biblical terms as they would have been understood by their authors, you will find some words herein that have different nuances or connotations than what you usually hear, such as *apocalyptic, forgiveness, sin, hell*, and *blessing*. At the same time, in basing this book primarily on the teachings of Jesus, I have tried to conform to what he said without "toning them down" to make his words "more reasonable." I believe he meant what he said, and that he meant for us to change our way of thinking, not to make his words conform to our thoughts and attitudes.

Your Notebook

Writing things down often helps one to learn, to remember and to achieve one's goals. In offering ways for you to carry out the spiritual practices in this book, I suggest you use a small notebook. Divide each page into four parts and make notes on each of the following practices: *forgiving, blessing, giving thanks* and *loving* (by acting). If you wish to make notes about *perceiving,* put them on separate pages at the beginning of your notebook. Notes about *praying* can be combined with those about *blessing.* As you enter your notes on each practice, you can compare what you have written concerning it from one entry to the next, as well as seeing what you have logged on a particular day. Date each day's entry, but do not feel compelled to make entries every day. How often you make an entry is your choice — every day, every week, or just from time to time.

When you come to the chapters on each of the six practices, you will find suggestions on what notes you can make in your notebook. Write whatever is helpful; you are not restricted to my suggestions.

The Mansion on the Hill

But [Jesus] said to him, "A certain man made a great supper, and he invited many people. And he sent his servant at the hour for supper to tell those who were invited, 'Come, for everything is ready now.' They all as one began to make excuses.

"The first said to him, 'I have bought a field, and I must go and see it. Please have me excused.'

"Another said, 'I have bought five yoke of oxen, and I must go try them out. Please have me excused.'

"Another said, 'I have married a wife, and therefore I cannot come.'

"That servant came, and told his lord these things. Then the master of the house, being angry, said to his servant, 'Go out quickly into the streets and lanes of the city, and bring in the poor, maimed, blind, and lame.'

"The servant said, 'Lord, it is done as you commanded, and there is still room.'

"The lord said to the servant, 'Go out into the high ways and hedges, and compel them to come in, that my house may be filled. For I tell you that none of those men who were invited will taste of my supper.'" (Luke 14:16-24, NHEB)

The parable of the feast requires some explanation because of its social context. All the excuses are unacceptable and senseless. The first person claims to have bought some land, sight unseen, which is now to be inspected. Those who do this nowadays can expect to gain title to worthless swamp land or wasted desert; the same was true then.

The second has to test some oxen. In biblical times, oxen were valuable animals for farming, but they had to be not only healthy, but correctly matched, so that the pair would pull in unison. No farmer in his right mind would buy a pair of oxen without first doing the test; to buy five pair without a test is the height of stupidity. The equivalent today would be to buy a car from the classifieds without knowing the make, mileage, or condition.

In the third case, a man claims to have just been married. However, in biblical times marriages were community events, widely known by everyone in advance of the event; since animals were butchered for the feast and meat could not be preserved overnight, the whole community was invited. And no one would ever compete with a wedding feast by inviting the same community to another big feast at the same time. This last excuse is the most offensive.

Finally, we have the command of the master to the servant, "make them come in." Some versions translate "make" as "force" or "compel." This sounds harsh until we understand social customs at the time this story was written. If it should ever happen that someone very rich should invite someone very poor, it was so much out of place that it was always the obligation of the poor to refuse the invitation. No matter how much the rich person would plead, the poor person would think, "This invitation is not for real; it is just a social gesture," and would keep on refusing. The only way for the one of high social rank to show that he or she truly and sincerely intended the invitation would be to use some kind of physical force.

I go because I'm sent, for I have orders to fulfill.
I represent the owner of the mansion on the hill.
The owner is a lover who's in love with everyone,
with every mother's daughter and every father's son.

I bear an invitation to a banquet and a feast.
All are welcome to come in, from greatest to the least.
Please join the fun and bring your friends; it is my owner's
        will.
So honor us and join us in the mansion on the hill.

Some I asked refused to come, and senseless reasons gave.
With bad intent and sad excuse their road to hell they pave.
And so in hedgerows and in alleys, in each corner, by each
        brook,
for each and every one who'll come I search and hunt and
        look.

So will you come to share the feast, to drink and eat your
        fill?
Will you come to dinner at the mansion on the hill?
Do you think you must refuse — it's too good to be true?
Does dining in a palace seem a dream that's not for you?

You hesitate because you know there must be some
　　mistake?
No gift to bring? No clothes to wear? And which path
　　should you take?
Then clearly understand just where your thinking has gone
　　wrong:
the mansion is your one true home, the place where you
　　belong.

Perhaps you've never met a mansion dweller face to face.
Perhaps you fear you lack the learning and the social grace
to be at ease with one whose riches far surpass
the earnings of your neighbors and your friends and social
　　class.

If it seems hard to see yourself within a mansion's walls,
if you think you're out of place to walk down royal halls,
then you must look within yourself, to see how much
　　you're worth.
To see the future, view the past — recall your royal birth.

God's kingdom is outside you, and it also is within.
To see outside, your inner vision's where you must begin.
The inner mansion of your heart let God's own Spirit fill.
You need no other path to reach the mansion on the hill.

Part I

Perceiving

1

How Early Christians Saw Themselves

In 1972, the Catholic Church reformed the way converts were to be received by promulgating the Rite of Christian Initiation of Adults (RCIA). This was a modern version of the ancient practice of the catechumenate, the word *catechumen* designating a prospective convert. Throughout the process, which could take place over a year or more, the catechumen would undergo instructions and rituals expressing the change one would experience through baptism.

The RCIA brought into its rituals various aspects of the ceremonies in the early centuries of Christianity. This restoral of ancient ceremonies includes two practices that reveal much about how early Christians viewed themselves, the pagans, and their relationship with God: (1) the exorcism of converts, and (2) the presentation of the Lord's Prayer.

Exorcism is the ritual by which the devil is cast out of someone. In the baptismal ceremony it is accompanied by the catechumen's renunciation of Satan and all his works. It was always done near the beginning of the ceremony and is included (in the Catholic Church and some others) in the baptism of infants as well as that of adults.

The Lord's Prayer was taught to a catechumen several weeks prior to being baptized. In the RCIA it generally occurs on the fifth Sunday in Lent. For infants, the Lord's Prayer is said after the baptism.

There are no traces of these two elements in the beginning of Christianity. They had to have been added later, and not merely as an enhancement, but as a necessary element to illustrate how Christians interpreted baptism to change one's relationship with God. Converts to Christianity had to be exorcised, because Christians believed they were bound to Satan — under his influence and the dominion of evil. Infants, too, were born in servitude to the devil and had to have the devil driven out of them.

By being taught the Lord's Prayer, the catechumen learned that baptism delivered one from the power of evil and became a child of God, no longer a slave of the devil. Through baptism one could call God "Father," which was impossible while still under the dominion of Satan.

The church, then, was the community of the elect, of God's children, of the purified. The pagans — those outside the church — were children of evil, of darkness, and of Satan. The church embodied truth and goodness; others embraced falsehood and evil. We cannot imagine a starker contrast between "us" and "them." Each group thought itself superior to the other; consequently, finding common ground between the two became impossible. There was tolerance, but not true acceptance.

Two questions arise from the world view of early Christians: (1) Where did this pessimistic view of non-Christians come from? And (2) How does this view conform to what Jesus taught? We will consider these questions in the following chapters.

2

The Pessimistic View of Gentiles

The view of Gentiles as sin-filled reprobates was widespread in first century Judea. Although Jews had to associate with Gentiles in affairs of commerce and politics, they were forbidden to intermarry or share food with them. A Gentile was never equal to a Jew, nor was total equality attained by a Gentile upon conversion to Judaism. A convert, known as a *proselyte,* became a real Jew, but was never equal to a descendant of Abraham. Since Jews believed that promiscuity among Gentiles was the norm, they deemed all Gentile children as almost certainly illegitimate. Consequently, if a proselyte's children were born before their father's conversion (i.e., while a Gentile), they could not (since they were likely illegitimate) inherit from their father. After the destruction of the temple, and probably before as well, a proselyte was regarded as without mother or father or any other relationship.

Women proselytes could not marry a priest unless converted before the age of three. There were also restrictions on a proselyte's right to hold some civic offices.[1]

The principal claim to Judaic superiority over Gentiles arose from the pride in being a "son of Abraham." Those who could trace their lineage back to Abraham claimed a share in the merits of their ancestors, so that they were made acceptable to God by the prayers and merits of their forefathers. Without this ancestry, proselytes were deprived of this benefit. Through ancestral prayers and merits, ethnic Jews could appease God, atone for their sins, and be guaranteed a place in the eternal kingdom of God. Proselytes were on their own, without the help of ancestors.[2] Thus the disparagement of Gentiles carried over to proselytes because of their Gentile ancestry.

Jews perceived all Gentiles, as worshipers of false gods, to be under the domain of evil, a cosmic power controlling the world and at times personified as an evil spirit. They were thought to be so lacking in sexual morality that all were to be treated as illegitimate.

This condescending view of Gentiles was expressed by the apostle Paul in his letter to the Romans, chapter 1, verses 18-32. He depicts God as angry over the irreligious and evil spirit of those who ignore the truth of God's power in creation by turning to false worship. Because these people had turned to serving creatures (i.e., idols), God abandoned (delivered up or handed over)

---

[1] Joachim Jeremias, *Jerusalem in the Time of Jesus,* Fortress Press, Philadelphia, 1975, pp. 320-354.

[2] *Ibid.,* pp. 320-354.

them to their corrupt passions and behavior. Paul enumerates a number of the crimes these people are guilty of — practices that were well known among the Gentiles in the Roman Empire.

> So, too, there is a revelation from heaven of the divine wrath against every form of ungodliness and wickedness on the part of those people who, by their wicked lives, are stifling the truth. This is so, because what can be known about God is plain to them; for God himself has made it plain. For ever since the creation of the universe God's invisible attributes — his everlasting power and divinity — are to be seen and studied in his works, so that people have no excuse; because, although they learned to know God, yet they did not offer him as God either praise or thanksgiving. Their speculations about him proved futile, and their undiscerning minds were darkened. Professing to be wise, they showed themselves fools; and they transformed the glory of the immortal God into the likeness of mortal humans, and of birds, and beasts, and reptiles.

> Therefore God abandoned them to impurity, letting them follow the cravings of their hearts, until they dishonored their own bodies; for they had substituted a lie for the truth about God, and had reverenced and worshiped created things more than the Creator, who is to be praised for ever. Amen. That, I say, is why God abandoned them to degrading passions. Even the women among them perverted the natural use of their bodies to the unnatural; while the men, disregarding that for which women were intended by nature, were consumed with passion for one another. Men indulged in vile practices with men, and incurred in their own persons the inevitable penalty for their perverseness.

> Then, as they would not keep God before their minds, God abandoned them to depraved

thoughts, so that they did all kinds of shameful
things. They reveled in every form of wickedness,
evil, greed, vice. Their lives were full of envy, murder, quarrelling, treachery, malice. They became
back-biters, slanderers, impious, insolent, boast-
ful. They devised new sins. They disobeyed their
parents. They were undiscerning, untrustworthy,
without natural affection or pity. Well aware of
God's decree, that those who do such things deserve to die, not only are they guilty of them themselves, but they even applaud those who do
them. (Romans 1:18-32, OEB)

Paul's reasoning can be summarized in two remarkable principles or beliefs about the relationship between God and humanity: (1) God so abandons those
who do not render worship and gratitude that they fall
into the worst degrading kinds of behavior. (2) Those
who fall into the worst degrading kinds of behavior do so
because they do not worship the one true God.

It would be hard to find any theologians today,
Christian or otherwise, who believe that those who do
not worship the God of the Jews and Christians are nec-
essarily reprobate sinners, or that those who are guilty
of the worst crimes are sinners because they do not worship the true God.

Where, then, did the early Christians get their pessimistic attitude toward Gentiles? First, it was the view
of Jews in the first century, and then it was delivered to
the first converts by the apostle Paul. But was this the
view that Jesus embraced?

3

How Jesus Saw Humanity

The predominant view of humanity among Jews in the first century was one of moral superiority over the Gentiles, whom they believed to be corrupt through and through. This belief was passed on to early Christian converts, who determined that pagans were under the dominion of evil. Rather than assume that Jesus shared this outlook, we will examine his teachings. But first, we take a close look at his audience, to see how his hearers understood his message.

Jesus spent most of his public ministry in Galilee. He was raised in Nazareth in Galilee, and his apostles and disciples were Galileans. To understand the people of Galilee and how they were different than most other Jews, we examine their history.

We start with the Greek king Antiochus IV Epiphanes, who banned Jewish religion and customs in order to turn the Jews into a Greek society. In 167 BCE he dedicated the Jerusalem temple to the Greek god Zeus. This desecration of the temple, called by the book of Daniel the abomination of desolation, ignited the Maccabean Revolt. After Antiochus V rescinded the edict of his father, the temple was rededicated. Even so, the rebellion continued under the Maccabean family and their successors, known as the Hasmoneans.

Judah, at that time just a small area in the center of what is now Israel, soon gained its freedom to practice its religion and customs. In 134 BCE, John Hyrcanus I gained power and immediately expanded his kingdom by conquering Idumaea to the south along with Samaria and parts of Transjordan. In so doing, however, he disregarded the principle of religious freedom and tolerance for which the first Maccabean patriots fought and died. John Hyrcanus destroyed the Samaritan temple on Mount Gerizim and allowed the Gentile Idumaeans to remain in their homes only if they were circumcised and converted to Judaism. They had little choice but to become Jews.

In 104 BCE, John Hyrcanus I was succeeded by his son Aristobulus, who quickly conquered the southern part of Iturea and the Golan to the north. The newly acquired portion of Iturea became known as Galilee. Aristobulus followed in the footsteps of his father by letting the inhabitants of Galilee stay in their homes only if they converted to Judaism. The territory of Galilee thus became a population of Gentile converts.

Herod the Great provides a typical example of how first century Jews viewed those not of Abrahamitic lineage, including proselytes and their descendants. His father Antipater was an Edomite converted to Judaism in the second century BCE. His mother was not a Jew, but from the Arab kingdom of Nabataea. Herod, though, was a practicing Jew. He married into the Hasmonean family, and began the construction of the massive new temple in Jerusalem, but failing to win over the Jewish populace. His ancestry was Gentile instead of from Abraham, making his claim to be king illegitimate.

The same second-class citizenship was the automatic lower rank bestowed on all those territories conquered by John Hyrcanus I and Aristobulus: Idumea, Samaria, Golan, and Galilee, the land in which Jesus spent most of his public life. Galileans, even though Jews, could not claim Abraham as their father.

We cannot underestimate how superior Jews with an Abrahamitic lineage felt. In 458 BCE, when the priest and scribe Ezra returned to Jerusalem after the exile, he discovered that many of the Jews had taken Gentile wives. Under his direction the men had to dismiss their wives and children. They were simply sent away to fend for themselves without concern for their welfare. The only thing that mattered was that the blood line from Abraham be kept pure. After the time of Ezra, Jews kept careful records of their ancestry, in order to prove their blood line was not contaminated.

John the Baptist railed against the arrogance of those who took comfort in their heritage. He warned them against saying, "Our father is Abraham."

> But when John saw many of the Pharisees and Sadducees coming to receive his baptism, he said to them, "You children of snakes! Who has prompted you to seek refuge from the coming judgment? Let your life, then, prove your repentance; and do not think that you can say among yourselves 'Abraham is our ancestor,' for I tell you that out of these stones God is able to raise descendants for Abraham!" (Matthew 3:7-10, OEB)

The Galileans could only feel second best to ethnic Jews, since they lacked the all-important claim to being children of Abraham. It is against this background that we visualize the amazement among the Galileans who first heard Jesus tell them to call God "Our Father."[3] For some one hundred thirty years — all the time since their ancestors had been forced to embrace Judaism — these people had been forced to live as a lower social caste, since they could never claim Abraham as their father. Now, by teaching them a simple prayer, they suddenly realized that their genealogy made no difference: God was their Father! It is striking that those whom Jesus chose as his apostles were Galileans and therefore not descendants of Abraham.[4]

The word Jesus used for "father" is striking. The Aramaic *abba* is better translated as "dad" or "daddy," since it is the first word a toddler used to address one's father. This word does not indicate God's gender, but our intimacy with God — a relationship like what we enjoy with our own parents.

Because Jesus was teaching Galileans, the Lord's Prayer cannot be labeled a "Christian" prayer. The Galileans were not Christians; Christianity did not exist at the time Jesus practiced his ministry. The practice of first century Christians of formally handing over the Lord's Prayer at the time of baptism lacks any foundation in the way Jesus taught it in the Gospels.

The apostle Paul added a new twist to Jesus's teaching by calling his converts God's children by adoption.[5] His thinking seems to be that before Jesus came we were not God's children, but through Jesus Christ we

---

[3] Matthew 6:9-15; Luke 11:2-4.
[4] Mark 1:16-20; 2:13-14; 14:70; Acts 2:7.
[5] Romans 8:15; Galatians 4:5; Ephesians 1:5.

have been adopted. To interpret Paul, we must understand his audience. Among the Romans an adopted child was held in greater esteem than a natural born child, because a child by adoption was specifically chosen. The best way Paul could express God's love was to put it in terms of adoption. Paul wanted to show the difference between those who had embraced Jesus and those who had not; he made adoption — becoming God's children by God's deliberate choice — the difference between the two.

Whatever may have been Paul's theology on spiritual adoption or his reasons for expressing it as he did, we find no hint of his interpretation in Jesus's teaching. Neither do we find in the Gospels the same disparaging view of pagans as that voiced by Paul. On two occasions, Jesus is said to have healed Gentiles: (1) the healing of the son of a Roman centurion,[6] and (2) the healing of the daughter a Canaanite woman.[7] Since these miracles run counter to the prevalent Jewish attitude toward Gentiles, they are likely to have a basis in historical fact, especially since Jesus acted, as he did in all his healings, only out of concern for the petitioner and desiring nothing in return, not even a conversion to Judaism.

Jesus's image of our relationship with the Father stands out boldly in the parable of the prodigal son.[8] The younger son persuades his father to give him his share of his inheritance, which he takes with him and squanders in a far off country. After a miserable existence, suffering famine so much that he wished he could eat some of the food he had to give to pigs, he reached a turning point.

---

[6] Matthew 8:5-13; Luke 7:1-10.
[7] Matthew 15:21-28; Mark 7:24-30.
[8] Luke 15:11-32.

"He even longed to satisfy his hunger with the bean-pods on which the pigs were feeding; and no one gave him anything. But, when he came to himself, he said 'How many of my father's hired servants have more bread than they can eat, while here am I starving to death! I will get up and go to my father, and say to him "Father, I sinned against heaven and against you; I am no longer fit to be called your son; make me one of your hired servants."'" (Luke 15:16-19, OEB)

To clarify the literal translation of Luke 15:17, "he came to himself," some biblical versions have "he came to his senses." However this verse is translated, the meaning is clear from his decision to return to his father.

Verse seventeen is the central verse of the parable, describing the conversion of the prodigal son. Before that point, he had forgotten who he was. His conversion comes when he remembers he was his father's son. He was *reborn* by *remembering* who he was, who he had always been, and who he always would be.

When Jesus taught his disciples and the Galileans to call God "Father," he was revealing to all, including us, who we are, who we always have been, and who we always will be: children of a loving God, our abba, our daddy. When we say we are reborn, our *rebirth* is a process of *remembering* who we are and who we have always been.

In the Old Testament the Israelites used several names to address God. Jesus used none of them, not even "Creator," frequently used by many Christians today. This omission is one more reason to reject the thought that Jesus ever thought of our relationship with God as one of adoption.

When we refer to God as Creator, we project an image of our being made out of nothing, totally dependent upon God, but also totally separate from God. To be spiritually adopted by God, then, is for God to act *as if* we are children or to *pretend* that we are really children. Adoption is always a legal fiction.

To be an adopted child of God is comparable to being a Pinocchio, made of wood and then turned into a real girl or boy. But after this miraculous change, the newly formed girl or boy could never claim to be a real daughter or son, even through adoption. Geppetto, the toymaker, could never claim that Pinocchio was his real son after he became a real boy; he could only pretend, or act *as if*, this were true.

There is no rite, ceremony or behavior that we can undertake that will make God pretend that we are God's children. Jesus told us to call God "Father," because God is already our Father and we are already God's children. We always were, and we always will be.

Because we fall into the snare of judging on appearances, we fail to *perceive* what magnificent and powerful gifts we are. In John 10:34 Jesus quotes Psalm 82:6:

> I said, "You are gods,
> all of you are sons of the Most High.
> (Psalm 82:6, NHEB)

We are all children of the same God, regardless of nationality, religion, race, gender, sexual preference, or anything else. We need to look within and remember who we are.

Jesus tells us,

> "You are salt for the world. But if salt becomes tasteless, how can it be made salty again? It is no longer good for anything, but is thrown away, and trampled underfoot. It is you who are the light of the world. A town that stands on a hill cannot be hidden. People do not light a lamp and put it under a basket, but on the lamp-stand, where it gives light to everyone in the house. Let your light

so shine before the eyes of others so that, seeing your good actions, they will praise your Father who is in heaven." (Mathew 5:13-16, OEB)

We are light, we are gods, we are children of God — powerful spiritual beings. Our spiritual light is not meant to be hidden, but to enlighten others. We are not receptacles of God's love, but channels. Our light and love grows brighter and stronger only by sharing with others.

We are not our race, our religion, our work, our accomplishments, our mistakes, our possessions, our social position, or our misdeeds. We are God's children — we always were and we always will be. God has always loved us, and God always will love us — unconditionally.

Remember who you really are.

We may *observe* disunity, separation, and distinctions between ourselves and others. Jesus taught us the real truth and *meaning* that lies beneath what we see.

The other side of the coin is that everyone else — those in other nations, of other religions, of another race, of all genders — our friends and our enemies — those who agree with us and those who do not — all without exception are also children of God, the light of the world and the salt of the earth. It is not enough for us to *pretend* that this is true or to act *as if* it were true; we must accept our true identity as a fundamental truth.

4

Born or Created?

Among Christian churches there is general agreement on basic doctrines. Most accept the Nicene Creed proclaimed at the Council of Nicea in 325 CE; and nearly all will recite the Apostles' Creed, which lays out the doctrines of the Trinity, the divinity of Jesus, and his death and resurrection. Lacking in this consensus is any agreement on human nature.

Few Christians believe the materialistic (proposed by some scientists) view of humankind in which we are composed entirely of physical matter. This view proposes that consciousness is a product of a physical brain, and when someone dies, that person ceases to exist. Christians adhere to a belief in life after death. This belief can be reconciled with the absence of a human soul or spirit only by imagining that God re-creates each human person sometime after death (on the Day of the Judgment?).

More prevalent is the belief in a spiritual component of each human being, usually called a soul. The material body ceases to exist at death, whereas the soul, being spiritual, continues to exist.

Pope Pius XII took this belief a step further by teaching that God creates each human soul at the time of conception. This teaching was never officially defined as a revealed doctrine, as was done with the doctrines of the Immaculate Conception and the Assumption of Mary; but it was taught in a papal encyclical and is therefore among the official teachings of the Catholic Church.

Catholic belief is further expanded by the belief that a human being is not a total person without a physical body. At death, then, we are not complete persons and will not be until the resurrection of the body on the last day. The resurrection of the body is one of the articles of faith stated in the Apostles' Creed, and the Catholic Church has added the notion of being incomplete human persons to explain it.

Christians other than Catholics may give little thought to when God creates the human soul, but most likely would accept the belief that God does create souls. However, there is a growing belief that we are not our bodies; we are instead spiritual beings who happen to have a body during our earthly lifetime. For those holding this opinion there is no need for a bodily resurrection to get our human personhood back.

An implicit belief among most Christians is that God created all things — the world, the universe, all living beings, and all that exists outside of God — out of nothing. If so, then God and creation are so totally distinct that we have no way to explain how we can ever achieve unity with God. With this mindset, Christians easily came to believe that they alone had a unique access to God's love, while pagans, separated from God and without the privileges of Christians, were totally distinct and separated from God, and as a result, sinful and corrupt.

Christian Holiness versus Pagan Corruption

The theory of the apostle Paul in the first chapter of Romans, in which he advocated the belief that pagans were corrupt because they worshiped false gods, never took hold among later Christians. The Christian population in the Roman Empire came from pagan converts, and Christians believed that the whole human race was born into a sinful condition from which they were delivered through baptism. Christians were saved not by turning away from false gods, but by being baptized.

This view of humankind's corrupt nature was explained by the invention of the doctrine of original sin, traced to Irenaeus, bishop of Lyon, and further enlarged by Augustine of Hippo. According to this doctrine all humanity shared in the sin of Adam, which was removed or forgiven in baptism.

The opposite of the state of sin was the holiness bestowed in baptism. Pagans could not acquire this holiness — or be released (or forgiven) from original sin — on their own power; baptism was necessary. (To escape this dilemma, theologians created the doctrines of baptism of desire and baptism of blood. We will not go into these topics here.) The primary reasoning for this involves the story of creation.

By reading into Genesis the doctrine of original sin, we are led to interpret the story of Adam and Eve in something like this: God created the world, including the first man and woman, out of nothing. Adam and Eve were created in a state of holiness as friends with God. Through the first sin, however, Adam lost the gift of holiness, which he could no longer pass on to his descendants.

To explain why the children of Adam and Eve could not become holy (or friends with God) without inheriting this gift, a theological explanation like this is given: The world and all humanity were created out of nothing, totally distinct from God. God is infinite; we are finite. Human beings and the universe in which we live are in the *natural* world. God is in the *supernatural* world. Everything in the natural or finite world is powerless to experience anything in the supernatural or infinite world by means of its own power.

Once the divine gift of holiness was lost, human beings could no longer retrieve it on their own. It had to be given to them all over again. Baptism was the remedy to restore us to God's love and friendship.

A new terminology was necessary to name what Christians had that non-Christians did not have. Theologians latched onto the word *grace*. In the New Testament this frequently used term meant "favor" or "benefit," and "thanks" in the plural. The Greek word the biblical authors used was *charis*, translated into Latin by *gratia*, from which the English word *grace* is derived. Some biblical translators have realized that "grace" is a poor translation of the Greek original; and in some cases, have put forward different wording. For example, the *New Jerusalem Bible* translates Luke 1:30 as "you have won God's favour," and in the *New Revised Standard Version* you find "you have found favor with God," instead of the traditional "full of grace." Today most who read the Bible are unaware that many English words do not have the meaning that the original authors intended.

If we look upon original sin as slavery to Satan, then it can be pictured as a real thing which we inherit. On the other hand, original sin was not a thing passed down from one generation to the next, but the *absence* of God's gift of love and friendship, resulting in everyone being born into this world at enmity with God. The gift of holiness or of God's love, newly named "grace," was a positive, created quality or attribute bestowed on human beings. Theologians described grace as a "created share in divine life." As such, it was beyond the reach of any human being by one's own power.

Grace was explained as a supernatural gift, since it bestowed a share in divine life, which is above the nature of human beings. Upon being baptized, one was said to be "in the state of (sanctifying) grace." Those without grace were "in the state of sin."

At baptism each catechumen was clothed with a white garment to signify one's new supernatural life, called the "state of grace" (or of "sanctifying grace"). This elevation in one's nature did not guarantee that a Christian would automatically attain heaven. Christians were able to sin after baptism, and they did sin, at times seriously. By the fourth century the response of the Church to fallen members was severe. Grave sins were punished by excommunication, which removed the sinner from communion until the bishop removed the sanction, often not until years later. A second serious fall would repeat the penalty, not to be removed until one was near death.

The practical consequences of this penitential practice were enormous. Potential converts postponed their baptism as long as possible, since baptism removed not only original sin, but all personal sins as well. Many endeavored to put off baptism until they were at death's door. Constantine, for example, was baptized on his deathbed.

Why Grace Does Not Work

The doctrine of sanctifying grace was invented to explain how we human beings can bridge the gap between our natural (or finite) nature and the domain of the supernatural (or infinite). To achieve any connection or union with God, we need supernatural help. Grace, even though called "a created share in the divine life," cannot enable a human being to achieve union with God, since grace is also a created gift. If we, as human beings, cannot achieve union with God on our own because we are finite and created, then neither can grace, since it, too, is finite and created.

The only explanation of how we can be united to God lies in Jesus's teaching that we are children of God. As spiritual beings, we were not created; we were *born*. However we express this truth in our limited human vocabulary, we say that God is both our Father and our Mother; God gave birth to us; we are born from God. This is what it means to be children of God.

Recall that Jesus said we are gods.[9] We are spiritual beings of light. By our spiritual nature we all have within us a spark of the divine. As God's children we live in the natural world and supernatural world at the same time, although the idea of natural and supernatural might best be forgotten as a false distinction.

Sanctifying grace, then, is a contradiction that does not exist and is not needed.

Our limited powers of observation do not perceive the true meaning of who we are. Jesus has given us the true meaning of life in teaching us that we are one with the Father as God's children.

---

[9] John 10:34.

33

Returning to What Jesus Taught

What Jesus taught was far simpler than the contradictory and pessimistic distinctions created by theologians centuries later:

1. Although first century Jews looked upon Gentiles as sinful, they were still just as human as the Jews; and their corruption was attributed to their sinful actions. Gentiles were believed to be equally as capable of acting justly as the Jews, and they were never thought to be incomplete human beings, lacking the power to do good.

2. Jesus preached that we are God's children. His hearers were Galileans living at a time before Christianity began and before Christian missionaries began baptizing Gentiles.

3. As God's children we are already connected to God. Jesus never taught that we have to do something extra or receive something extra to become a child of God.

4. If we, because of our finite human nature, are incapable of union with God, then one more finite created gift — whether you call it sanctifying grace or simply a divine favor — will be not able to give us that power. In other words, if we cannot do something because we are finite and created, then neither can any kind of grace enable us, since it is also finite and created.

5

The Spiritual Practice of Perceiving

The spiritual practice of *perceiving* is the first step on our path to unconditional love. We begin by seeing ourselves and God as Jesus taught us, especially in the Lord's Prayer. Nowhere in the Gospels do we find Jesus calling God anything other than Father — not Creator or Father Almighty (as in the Apostles' Creed), nor by any of the names used in the Hebrew Scriptures. *Abba* (*Daddy*) is the only word he used.

God loves even the worst sinner; and if God did not see sinners as lovable, God could not love them or forgive them. The same is true for you. You cannot love someone if you do not see that person as lovable. As a result, the practice of *perceiving* is the foundation for all other spiritual practices.

By *perceiving,* we remind ourselves that we are all lovable in God's eyes.

So Jesus told them this parable — "Who among you who has a hundred sheep, and has lost one of them, does not leave the ninety-nine out in the open country, and go after the lost sheep until he finds it? And, when he has found it, he puts in on his shoulders rejoicing; and, on reaching home, he calls his friends and his neighbors together, and says 'Come and rejoice with me, for I have found my sheep which was lost.' So, I tell you, there will be more rejoicing in heaven over one outcast who repents, than over ninety-nine religious people, who have no need to repent." (Luke 15:3-7, OEB)

Perceiving as Jesus taught us can be part of your daily prayers. Remind yourself of who others are as you pray for them. This can become a habit practiced throughout the day. When you are visiting friends, shopping, in the gym, watching the news on television, seeing children on the playground, or catching a glimpse of a beggar on the street, remind yourself that all are God's children. Visualize them as spiritual beings of light. See them as your sisters and brothers.

Since all of humanity is born from the same Father-Mother God, we are all one family. We all have the divine with us. We are one with each other and one with God; our oneness is who we are. Remind yourself frequently of your oneness, because your physical vision sees only individual, separate human beings

Do not be discouraged if you find it difficult to see someone, maybe a hardened criminal or someone who has abused you, as a child of God. Just pray for help in seeing in everyone the divine spark that makes them worth loving. Acknowledge that God sees everyone as lovable. You do not need to spend a long time in this prayer or in recalling that others are God's children. Make the practice short but frequent. You can also repeat biblical verses, such as "You are the light of the world" or "You are the salt of the earth."

To see more clearly what you mean to God, write down what you would want most for your children or others close to you. For example, you may want them independent and respect their choices and free will. You may want them to be happy, but does that mean an abundance of possessions? How would you want them to treat the poor and underprivileged? Does it make a difference whether they show love for others?

Not all children are loyal to their parents or even love them. Write down how you think a loving mother or father would respond.

Many think that the worst tragedy a parent can experience is the death of a child. Write down how you think God sees the death of his or her children.

Perceiving is a practice of reminding ourselves that we are all lovable and that God loves everyone. As a spiritual *practice*, it is something we must repeat over and over to make it a consistent habit.

Your Notebook

If you wish to make notes for *perceiving*, I suggest that you place them on separate pages in the beginning of your notebook.

Like Mother, Like Daughter

Like Father, Like Son

"You have heard that it was said — 'You must love your neighbor and hate your enemy.' But what I tell you is this: love your enemies, and pray for those who persecute you, so that you may become children of your Father who is in heaven; for he causes his sun to rise on bad and good alike, and sends rain on the righteous and on the unrighteous. For, if you love only those who love you, what reward will you have? Even the tax-gatherers do this! And, if you only welcome your brothers and sisters, what are you doing more than others? Even the Gentiles do this! You, then, must become perfect — as your heavenly Father is perfect." (Matthew 5:43-48, OEB)

The following poem is based on Matthew 5:43-48, which states God's love for the just and the unjust, and especially on verse 48, which commands us to be perfect like our heavenly Father. It also reflects the Lord's Prayer. Note that in the last stanza one's human parents are no longer being referenced.

You tell us who your mother is, for we see her in you.
You can't hide who your father is; he's there in all you do.

Even at the age of three, you tell us who you are.
You have your mother's eyes, you see, that twinkle like a
     star.
Your chin comes from your father, but you have your
     mother's hair.
Your laughter and your smile with both your mom and dad
     you share.

When dad or mommy play with you and call you by your
     name,
you know at once your parents' voice and love to play their
     game.
All you have to do is laugh — your parents' heart you've
     won.
You are your mother's daughter, you are your father's son.

You tell us who your mother is, for we see her in you.
You can't hide who your father is; he's there in all you do.

You're older now, and now at school, away from home all
     day,
but we see someone else in you, in how you act and play.
Look at how you swing your bat — your father's taught
     you well;
and how you sing and dance is from your mother, we can
     tell.

You may not eat your turnips when you're told they're
    good for you,
but "Please" and "Thank you" echo what your parents say
    and do.
Just be yourself, in work or play, and when the day is done,
you're still your mother's daughter, you're still your
    father's son.

You tell us who your mother is, for we see her in you.
You can't hide who your father is; he's there in all you do.

You've left the nest, you're on your own; now ponder how
    you choose.
How do you vote? How do you pray? What are your don'ts
    and do's?
You help to clear the neighbor's snow as daddy used to do.
You bring a supper for the sick, as mommy taught you to.

You teach your children not to lie, not to cheat or steal,
for that's the way that you were taught, to other's feelings
    feel.
Your parents taught you, do to others as to you'd be done.
You are your mother's daughter, you are your father's son.

You tell us who your Mother is, for we see Her in you.
You can't hide who your Father is; He's there in all you do.

Ah, but there are those of you whose father is unknown.
It may be that your mother died before you'd hardly grown.
Some fathers have abused a child — you may be one of
    those.
Some mothers make their children cry — just why, nobody
    knows.

It doesn't really matter who you are or where you've been.
Your parents may have taught you love, they may have
    taught you sin.
What matters most is not your past, what others did to you,
but how your enemies you see, and how you others view.

Give love to those who hate you, to those who've caused
    you grief.
When pierced by lance of hatred, only love will give relief.
So pray, "O God, forgive them, for they know not what
    they've done."
You are your Mother's daughter, you are your Father's son.

Part II

Forgiving

6

Jesus on Forgiveness

Christians of all sects have many points of agreement. Surprisingly, forgiveness of sin is not one of them. Catholics and Orthodox disagree with Protestants by insisting on the need for confession of sins to a priest. While there is common ground on the need for sorrow for one's sins, the Catholic position is far more complex, and it can be illustrated by examining the prayer taught to children in preparation for confession and first communion, the act of contrition (or sorrow). This is the traditional version:

> O my God, I am heartily sorry for having offended Thee, and I detest all my sins, because I dread the loss of heaven, and the pains of hell, but most of all because they offend Thee, my God, Who are all good and deserving of all my love. I firmly resolve, with the help of Thy grace, to confess my sins, to do penance, and amend my life. Amen.

This prayer is actually a theological statement in the format of a prayer, from which we derive these beliefs about forgiveness of sin:

1. Sorrow is necessary to receive forgiveness.
2. We should strive to be sorry because our sins offend God.
3. We need to be sorry at least because we fear the loss of heaven and the sufferings of hell.
4. We must firmly resolve not to sin again.
5. We must confess our sins (to a priest).
6. We must do penance or some tasks to make up for our sins.

Catholic theology about forgiveness is still more complicated than what is stated in the act of contrition. Sorrow because our sins offend God is called perfect contrition. If someone is dying without being able to confess to a priest, perfect contrition is sufficient to be forgiven; this is also true for those who are not Christian or do not believe in confession. However, sorrow out of fear of divine punishment, called imperfect contrition, is not sufficient for forgiveness in the same circumstances.

Although the Catholic Church teaches that all grave sins must be confessed, such sins are still forgiven as soon as one has perfect contrition. If one has only imperfect sorrow, forgiveness is not granted unless one receives a sacrament — usually confession (sacrament of reconciliation); but any other sacrament, such as baptism, confirmation, or anointing of the sick will suffice.

Some Protestants add a different requirement for forgiveness, at least in one's initial conversion: the acceptance of Jesus Christ as one's personal Lord and Savior.

Among all Christians, to be sorry for one's transgressions is the essential ingredient for forgiveness. We teach siblings to apologize and say, "I'm sorry," whenever one hurts another. In our court system, the word *sorrow* is often replaced by a term such as "remorse," but the meaning is the same.

The notion of sorrow for sin is absent from the Gospels. John the Baptist warned the Pharisees and Sadducees coming for baptism to do works showing true repentance[10]; but the word *repentance*, found in nearly every English version of the New Testament, is an inadequate translation of the Greek word *metanoia*, which means a "change of mind" or a "change in one's way of thinking." It is derived from two Greek words, *meta*, "change," and *nous*, mind. The connotation of sorrow is not to be read into the original Greek word which translators turn into the word *repentance*.

The Parable of the Unjust Steward

We cannot understand Jesus's teachings on forgiveness without changing our way of thinking. When he spoke about forgiveness, it was always in terms of what we must give (practice) rather than what we need to receive.

> Then Peter came up, and said to Jesus, "Master, how often am I to forgive someone who wrongs me? As many as seven times?" But Jesus answered, "Not seven times, but seventy times seven." (Matthew 18:21-22, OEB)

In other words, one must keep on forgiving. Then he expanded his answer in the parable of the unjust steward:

---

[10] Matthew 3:7-8.

[Jesus] answered, "Therefore the kingdom of heaven may be compared to a king who wished to settle accounts with his servants. When he had begun to do so, one of them was brought to him who owed him ten thousand bags of gold; and, as he could not pay, his master ordered him to be sold towards the payment of the debt, together with his wife, and his children, and everything that he had. The servant threw himself down on the ground before him and said 'Have patience with me, and I will pay you all.' The master was moved with compassion; and he let him go, and forgave him the debt.

"But, on going out, that same servant came upon one of his fellow servants who owed him a hundred silver coins. Seizing him by the throat, he said 'Pay what you owe me.' His fellow servant threw himself on the ground and begged for mercy. 'Have patience with me,' he said, 'and I will pay you.'

"But the other would not, but went and put him in prison until he should pay his debt. When his fellow servants saw what had happened, they were greatly distressed, and went to their master and laid the whole matter before him. So the master sent for the servant, and said to him 'You wicked servant! When you begged me for mercy, I forgave you the whole of that debt. Shouldn't you, also, to have shown mercy to your fellow servant, just as I showed mercy to you?'

"Then his master, in anger, handed him over to the jailers, until he should pay the whole of his debt. So, also, will my heavenly Father do to you, unless each one of you forgives his brother or sister from your heart." (Matthew 18:23-35, OEB)

The parable's message is simple: God freely forgives and expects us to freely forgive — without count —

in return. The only obstacle to enjoying God's gift of forgiveness is to refuse to pass the gift of forgiveness on to others. We are not reservoirs of God's love and forgiveness, but *channels*.

The Lord's Prayer

The key to obtaining forgiveness could not be stated more clearly than what Jesus taught in the Lord's Prayer: "And forgive us our debts, as we also forgive our debtors."[11] When we forgive (all) those who have injured us, God forgives us.

Jesus reinforced what he meant right after he teaches this prayer:

> "For, if you forgive others their offenses, your heavenly Father will forgive you also; but, if you do not forgive others their offenses, not even your Father will forgive your offenses." (Matthew 6:14-15, OEB)

The Woman Who Anoints Jesus's Feet

Luke tells of a woman, labeled as a sinner, who anoints the feet of Jesus.

> One of the Pharisees asked Jesus to dine with him, so Jesus went to his house and took his place at the table. Just then a woman, who was an outcast in the town, having heard that Jesus was eating in the Pharisee's house, brought an alabaster jar of perfume, and placed herself behind Jesus, near his feet, weeping. Then she began to make his feet wet with her tears, and she dried them with the hair of her head, repeatedly kissing his feet and anointing them with the perfume.

---

[11] Matthew 6:12, NHEB.

When the Pharisee who had invited Jesus saw this, he said to himself, "Had this man been 'the prophet,' he would have known who, and what sort of woman, this is who is touching him, and that she is an outcast." But, addressing him, Jesus said, "Simon, I have something to say to you."

"Pray do so, teacher," Simon answered; and Jesus began, "There were two people who were in debt to a moneylender; one owed five hundred silver coins, and the other fifty. As they were unable to pay, he forgave them both. Which of them, do you think, will love him the more?"

"I suppose," answered Simon, "it will be the man to whom he forgave the greater debt."

"You are right," said Jesus, and then, turning to the woman, he said to Simon, "Do you see this woman? I came into your house — you gave me no water for my feet, but she has made my feet wet with her tears and dried them with her hair. You did not give me one kiss, but she, from the moment I came in, has not ceased to kiss my feet. You did not anoint even my head with oil, but she has anointed my feet with perfume. So I tell you, her great love shows that her sins, many as they are, have been pardoned. One who is pardoned little loves little." Then he said to the woman, "Your sins have been pardoned."

The other guests began to say to one another, "Who is this man who even pardons sins?" But Jesus said to the woman, "Your faith has delivered you; go, and peace be with you." (Luke 7:36-50, OEB)

At the end of the story, Jesus says to those present, "So I tell you, her great love shows that her sins, many as they are, have been pardoned. One who is pardoned little loves little."[12] This translation is similar to what is found in the *New Revised Standard Version* of the Bible, one of the few versions which translates verse 47 as it is found in the Greek text. Most versions, including the older *Revised Standard Version,* translate this verse in the opposite sense, so that the woman is forgiven much because she has loved much. Their translators probably assumed they had to change the verse to make sense. However, our personal preference is not a sufficient reason to change the original text. We need instead to change our way of thinking: First comes God's forgiveness; then comes the woman's love.

The same is true for us. First we are forgiven; then we love in return.

The Lesson Jesus Taught

To understand Jesus's teaching about forgiveness we need to change our way of thinking, since it is the opposite of what we assume, as well as being far less complicated than what Christian churches teach and practice. God always forgives, even before we ask. If God expects us to forgive without limit, then certainly God does the same. We do nothing to win or deserve God's forgiveness or love. The only obstacle to receiving the benefit of God's forgiveness is failing to pass the gift on to others. Sorrow is neither the cause of nor the requirement for forgiveness, but our response to God.

---

[12] Luke 7:47, OEB. *The Jerusalem Bible* (Doubleday & Company, Garden City, New York, 1966) has the following comment in a note to verse 47: "Not, as is usually translated, 'her many sins are forgiven her because she has shown such great love'. The context demands the reverse: she shows so much affection because she has had so many sins forgiven."

7

The Apocalyptic Solution of the

Problem of Evil

The prophets of Israel, like us today, wrestled with the problem of evil. They believed their nation, as God's chosen people, was set apart from the Gentiles. The contrast was not just between good people and sinful people, but between a holy nation with the divine purpose of enlightening the way and those in darkness in need of enlightenment.

In the book of Isaiah, the prophet[13] writes as though he were the nation of Israel:

> Listen, islands, to me; and listen, you peoples,
> from far: the LORD has called me from the womb;

---

[13] Some Scripture authorities believe that the book of Isaiah had more than one author.

from the body of my mother has he made mention of my name: and he has made my mouth like a sharp sword; in the shadow of his hand, he has hidden me; and he has made me a polished arrow, in his quiver has he kept me close: and he said to me, "You are my servant; Israel, in whom I will be glorified." But I said, "I have labored in vain, I have spent my strength for nothing and vanity; yet surely the justice due to me is with the LORD, and my reward with my God."

Now says the LORD who formed me from the womb to be his servant, to bring Jacob again to him, and that Israel be gathered to him; for I am honorable in the eyes of the LORD, and my God has become my strength. And he says, "It is too light a thing that you should be my servant to raise up the tribes of Jacob, and to restore the preserved of Israel; I will also give you as a light to the nations, that you may bring salvation to the farthest place of the earth."

Thus says the LORD, the Redeemer of Israel, and his Holy One, to the one who is despised, to the abhorred of the nation, the servant of rulers: "Kings shall see and arise; princes, and they shall worship; because of the LORD who is faithful, even the Holy one of Israel, who has chosen you." Thus says the LORD, "In an acceptable time I have answered you, and in a day of salvation I have helped you; and I will preserve you, and give you as a covenant to the people, to raise up the land, to make them inherit the desolate heritage: saying to those who are bound, 'Come out.'; to those who are in darkness, 'Show yourselves.' (Isaiah 49:1-9, NHEB)

In this passage the prophet describes God's call to Israel before the nation's birth and the nation's sacred mission to be a light of salvation to the Gentiles. Israel's mouth as a sharp sword is symbolic of the mission to deliver God's message of salvation to the pagan nations.

God's Punishment of Israel

There were times when the Israelites proved unfaithful to God and turned to idolatry. When Jerusalem and its temple were destroyed and the Jews were taken into exile in Babylon, their sufferings were interpreted as direct punishment from God for their turning from God and breaking their covenant. Behind their reasoning are these convictions: (1) If they had been faithful to the covenant, God would have rewarded them and the nation would have flourished. (2) God is in immediate control of the earth and of all the good and evil that people experience.

Daniel and the Son of Man

By the second century BCE new ideas were injected into Jewish thinking about divine reward and punishment, expressed in the book of Daniel. Chapter 7 describes the succession of four kingdoms, symbolized by four beasts: (1) a lion with eagle's wings, (2) a bear with three tusks or ribs, (3) a leopard with four wings and four heads, and (4) a terrifying beast with ten horns; a small horn appeared, uprooting three others and displaying eyes like human eyes and a mouth talking arrogantly. Most interpreters of this chapter agree that the four beasts represent these kingdoms: (1) Babylon, (2) Media, (3) Persia, and (4) Greece, with the little horn being Antiochus Epiphanes IV, whose dedication of the temple to Zeus in 167 BCE was termed the abomination of desolation.

The vision of the four beasts is replaced by a fifth, in which someone like a son of man (i.e., a human being) comes on the clouds of heaven to the "Ancient of Days" (or the Ancient One), who confers upon him dominion, glory, and kingship over all peoples and nations.[14] Since the four beasts all represent nations, this final being, one like a son of man, would also represent a nation, which can only be Israel. Hence the vision of Daniel continues the theology of Isaiah, in which Israel will bring justice and salvation to the Gentiles.

Daniel adds new elements to explain how God is in control of human history. By predicting what was to come in specific periods ("weeks of years") and at "appointed times," Daniel hints that pagan rule is predetermined and will come to an end. That time as we know it will have an end is confirmed in chapter 12 by the novel prediction of the resurrection of the dead.

The book of Daniel, along with the book of Revelation, is labeled as apocalyptic literature. The word *apocalypse* is the Greek term for revelation or unveiling. Apocalyptic literature was widespread in the Jewish and early Christian world, with only the books of Daniel and Revelation gaining acceptance in the Christian canon. In the first two centuries BCE, the Jews felt ever increasing oppression as they came under Rome's dominion. They questioned why they were suffering, believing that they were faithful to their covenant. The book of Daniel helped to further the belief that God was about to end their misery by an immediate intervention in history, which would reverse Israel's fortune.

The Apocalyptic Culture of First Century Judea

The Gospels take the apocalyptic world view for granted. They assume that God is about to turn the world on its head, putting down the privileged and powerful while lifting up the poor and outcast to peace and honor: "But many who are first now will then be last, and those who

---

[14] Daniel 7:13-14.

are last will be first."[15] At the same time they assume that this cataclysmic reversal of fortunes will come in the immediate future.

Apocalypticism was not the only world view among the Jews, but it must have been the one in which Jesus grew up. It is also possible that he adopted it — or became firmly attached to it — through his association with John the Baptist.

Since the apocalyptic expectations of Jesus never came to pass, we must understand that the apocalyptic world view is to be considered a part of the culture in which Jesus expressed his message rather than an essential part of the message itself. The wider Jewish culture embraced the belief in a three-tiered universe with God reigning over the sky (a solid dome or firmament) and the demons and deceased confined to a domain below the earth. The apocalyptic world view, like this image of the universe (and like the Aramaic language), should be looked upon as the medium in which Jesus delivered his message rather than as part of the message.

As a result, Jesus's moral precepts do not depend for their validity upon the apocalyptic world view. His commands hold true regardless of the language, science, or world view in which they were pronounced. At the same time, apocalypticism did assert its influence on how Jesus expressed himself, and we must be aware of this as we attempt to understand the core of his preaching.

The Son of Man in the Gospels

The apocalyptic world view was common in first century Judea. We do not know how widespread it was held, but it stands out in the Gospels, beginning with the preaching

---

[15] Matthew 19:30, OEB.

of John the Baptist. In Matthew he harshly rebukes the
Pharisees and Sadducees who came for baptism and asks
them about who warned them to try to escape the coming wrath:

> But when John saw many of the Pharisees and
> Sadducees coming to receive his baptism, he
> said to them, "You children of snakes! Who has
> prompted you to seek refuge from the coming
> judgment?" (Matthew 3:7, OEB)

For him the end is imminent:

> "Already the axe is lying at the root of the trees.
> Therefore every tree that fails to bear good fruit
> will be cut down and thrown into the fire." (Mat-
> thew 3:10, OEB)

The preaching of John, like that of Jesus, was directed only to Jews, without reference to Gentiles. In Jesus's message, in contrast, we see that the apocalyptic
view had changed from the way it was presented in the
book of Daniel.

The theme of Jesus in the Synoptic Gospels (Matthew, Mark and Luke) is the coming of God's kingdom,
which is marked with these new characteristics:

1. God is going to immediately overturn the world
order in which evil is in control, and this is going to happen soon, even in the lifetimes of some who heard him.
He declared that some of those standing with him would
not "taste death" until they saw the kingdom of God coming in power.[16] This saying is considered authentic —
that is, close to Jesus's original words — because the
early Christians would not have invented a prediction
that had failed to come to pass.

---

[16] Mark 9:1.

2. The Son of Man, understood to be a distinct person instead of the nation of Israel, will be seated on a glorious throne, while the Twelve (i.e., the apostles) will judge the twelve tribes of Israel.[17] Since this promise included Judas, early Christians would not have created it; hence, it is believed to be close to Jesus's original words. The Last Judgment implies a belief in the resurrection of the dead at the end of time.

3. The Son of Man is a distinct personality from Jesus, who said that the Son of Man would be ashamed of anyone who was ashamed of Jesus and his message.[18] In the Gospels some passages refer to the Son of Man as other than Jesus, while others identify the two. After the Resurrection the followers of Jesus began to hope for his return, picturing him as the promised Son of Man. Although this title was quickly replaced by "Christ" or "Messiah" (Anointed One), the conflict between the various passages is explained by seeing those verses identifying Jesus with the Son of Man as modifications made by the first followers of Jesus.

Throughout the first century and beyond, Christians believed that Jesus would return soon and God would reverse the fortunes of the just and the unjust. After centuries had passed, it became apparent that the predictions of Jesus in the Gospels had failed to come to pass. Christians began to think of God's kingdom as far in the future. (In the petition, "Thy kingdom come," we still pray for God to eliminate evil in this world.)

The Apocalyptic Message of Paul

The apostle Paul taught the same apocalyptic message as in the Gospels, explaining how those who are still living

---

17 Matthew 19:27-28.
18 Mark 8:34-38.

when Jesus comes will not have an advantage over those
who have died:

> We don't want you to be ignorant, friends, about
> those who have passed to their rest. We don't
> want you to grieve like other people who have no
> hope. For, as we believe that Jesus died and rose
> again, so also we believe that God will bring, with
> Jesus, those who through him have passed to
> their rest. This we tell you on the authority of the
> Lord — that those of us who are still living at the
> coming of the Lord will not anticipate those who
> have passed to their rest. For, with a loud sum-
> mons, with the shout of an archangel, and with
> the trumpet-call of God, the Lord himself will
> come down from heaven. Then those who died in
> union with Christ will rise first; and afterward we
> who are still living will be caught up in the clouds,
> with them, to meet the Lord in the air; and so we
> will be for ever with the Lord. Therefore, comfort
> one another with what I have told you. (First
> Thessalonians 4:13-18, OEB)

Paul's words, "those of us who are still living at
the coming of the Lord," indicate his belief that some of
his hearers, and most likely he himself, would live to see
Jesus return.

The Didache

The *Didache* (*The Teaching of the Twelve Apostles*), written probably between 100 and 120 CE, about ten to thirty
years after the book of Revelation, was still anticipating
the second coming of the Lord, although the expectation
was no longer immediate.[19]

---

[19] *Didache,* Chapters 10:6, 16:7-8.

The Apocalyptic Message of Revelation

Toward the end of the first century CE a man named John on the island of Patmos wrote the most controversial book in the New Testament, *Revelation*. The Greek name of the book is *Apocalypse*; both names mean a revealing or unveiling. As the Greek name indicates, Revelation belongs to the genre of apocalyptic literature.

Until recently everyone thought John was a Gentile Christian. Behind this was the assumption that all who acclaimed Jesus as Messiah in the first century, especially New Testament authors, believed and taught exactly the same thing. Scripture scholars consistently interpreted the message of Revelation to fit Christian doctrines.

There are problems with such an assumption. One is that John of Patmos vehemently condemned the eating of food offered to idols,[20] whereas the apostle Paul allowed it.[21] Another is that John uses the term *synagogue* as well as *church*, and he rejects those who say they are Jews but are not.[22] He is familiar with the imagery of Isaiah, Jeremiah, Ezekiel and Daniel; and his contrasting the city of Rome with the heavenly Jerusalem does not fit the mentality of Gentile Christians, who were becoming more and more anti-Jewish and thought of Jerusalem only in terms of its destruction as a punishment for the rejection of the Messiah. Elsewhere in the New Testament, Christians are exhorted to obey civil law and pray for those in authority. For John, this attitude is unthinkable.

Consequently, the view gaining ground today is that John of Patmos accepted Jesus as the Messiah, but

---

[20] Revelations 2:14; 2:20.
[21] First Corinthians 8.
[22] Revelation 3:9.

was also a devout Jew. John sees a new heaven and a new earth, and the holy city, the new Jerusalem, descending from heaven as a bride dressed for her husband.[23] The bride is Jerusalem, the wife of the Lamb, with twelve foundations bearing the names of the twelve apostles.[24] His image is strictly Jewish, in opposition to the apostle Paul's description of the church as the wife of the (Gentile) church.[25] John also has the marriage of the Lamb and Jerusalem take place after evil has been conquered, whereas for Paul the union between Christ and the church is already present.

At the end of the book of Revelation he describes the new Jerusalem as measuring five hundred miles by five hundred miles, immensely larger than the fallen city of Rome.[26] The nations (Gentiles) walk by its light and their kings bring their glory into it. There is no temple in the city, for God and the Lamb are the temple.[27]

In chapter after chapter of Revelation, we have descriptions of disasters wrought upon the sinful Gentiles; yet at the end, the Gentiles walk in the light of the new Jerusalem. How did John expect this conversion of the pagans to come about?

Most commentators devote endless words pointing out and interpreting the plagues and disasters in Revelation. The Gentiles, however, were not overcome by any of these punishments. Instead, the only effective weapon was the sword from the mouth of the Messiah. The lesson here recalls the words from Isaiah, which symbolized how Israel would deliver God's message to bring salvation to the Gentiles.

---

[23] Revelation 21:1-2.
[24] Revelation 21:9-14.
[25] Ephesians 5:21-33.
[26] Revelation 21:15-16.
[27] Revelation 21:22-26.

In Revelation the armies representing evil, with the beast and the false prophet, are conquered. The kings of the earth gather at Armageddon, but no battle follows. There is no mention of armies of saints or of followers of the Lamb doing combat. The only weapon conquering evildoers is the sword from the mouth of the Lamb.

In Isaiah the sword is the mouth of the nation of Israel. John of Patmos modifies his image so that it is the Lamb — the Messiah — who conquers evil *in behalf of Israel*. The two images are not contradictory; the Messiah is the child of Israel, depicted in Revelation as the woman clothed with the sun.[28]

Revelation amplifies but continues the message of Isaiah: God wants all peoples to be saved, but evil is only conquered by truth, specifically by Jesus's message.

Summary of How God Deals with Evil

Throughout the Old Testament and the New it is clear that the Jews believed that God wanted the Gentiles to be saved through the nation of Israel. The book of Revelation demonstrates the uselessness of punishments to turn the Gentiles from evil. Instead, evil is overturned by the sword from the mouth of the Lamb — that is, the message of the Messiah.

Completely out of mind is the theological view of Paul, who preached the vicarious redemption of all humankind independent of the people of Israel. On the other hand, a fresh reading of Revelation uncovers a *contrasting but equally valid view* of who Jesus is and what he taught. For John, those washed in the blood of the Lamb are the *Jewish* followers, and the Lamb conquers the evil rampant among the Gentiles by the *sword of truth* that comes from his mouth.

---

[28] Revelation 12.

John of Patmos reminds us of the need to concentrate on *the sword of truth,* the message which Jesus delivered to the Galileans. The sword of truth reminds us to *heed what he taught.*

8

God and Sin

Jesus's Key to Understanding God

Jesus has given us the key to understanding sin from the divine perspective. In the Sermon on the Mount he encourages his hearers to ask God for what they need, for if they ask, they will receive; if they seek, they will find; if they knock, the door will be opened. He continues with a comparison between how we as parents give gifts and how God gives them. If a child asks for bread, we do not give a stone; or if a child asks for a fish, we do not give a snake. Finally, he states an all-important principle: if we, evil as we are, can give good gifts, then how much greater are the good gifts that our heavenly Father gives us:

> "Ask, and it will be given to you; search, and you will find; knock, and the door will be opened to

you. For the person who asks receives, the person who searches finds, and to the door will be opened to the person who knocks. Who among you, when their child asks them for bread, will give them a stone, or when they ask for a fish, will give them a snake? If you, then, wicked though you are, know how to give good gifts to your children, how much more will your Father who is in heaven give what is good to those who ask him!" (Matthew 7:7-11, OEB)

Jesus's principle can be stated thusly: Whatever good quality there is in any human being, God possesses in an infinitely greater measure.

We can also restate this principle: Whatever good Jesus commands us to do, God also does to an infinitely greater degree.

Once we understand, even in a small way, the love and goodness of God, we must then follow this norm Jesus has given us:

"You, then, must become perfect — as your heavenly Father is perfect." (Matthew 5:48, OEB)

God and Love for Enemies

Jesus tells us,

"You have heard that it was said — 'You must love your neighbor and hate your enemy.' But what I tell you is this: love your enemies, and pray for those who persecute you, so that you may become children of your Father who is in heaven; for he causes his sun to rise on bad and good alike, and sends rain on the righteous and on the unrighteous." (Matthew 5:43-45, OEB)

If we are to love our enemies, then does not God do the same? Although it may seem common for some to turn away from God by unjust acts, it is hard to conceive of persons deliberately becoming enemies of God. Nevertheless, if there are such persons, God still love them.

How are we to react when someone harms us? Our common tendency is to react in kind, to fight back, or to retaliate. This is the opposite of what Jesus wants.

> "You have heard that it was said — 'An eye for an eye and a tooth for a tooth.' But I say to you that you must not resist those who wrong you; but, if anyone strikes you on the right cheek, turn the other to them also. If someone sues you for your shirt, let them have your cloak as well. If you are forced to carry a soldier's pack for one mile, carry it two. Give to anyone who asks and, if someone wants to borrow from you, do not turn them away." (Matthew 5:38-42, OEB)

If we are commanded not to retaliate, God does not retaliate either. No matter what crimes one commits against God, God does not strike out and punish. God does not "press charges." God "turns the other cheek" to an infinitely greater and more loving degree than we do. Jesus says that we are to forgive without limit ("seventy times seven"[29]), then does not God do the same, and even more generously?

Sin and God's Response

To understand how God responds to sin, we have to know the several ways in which sin can be understood: (1) a transgression of divine law or the divine will; (2) an offense against reason or what one believes to be good; (3) an offense against God. We will approach sin in the third sense, understood as a serious crime often thought to break one's relationship with God.

---

[29] Matthew 18:22.

If by sinning we offend God, how does God take the offense? Being offended has been experienced by everyone, and a little introspection reveals that taking offense when injured is always a *personal choice*. If someone says something innocent about us, we can choose to take offense even if no insult was intended. Conversely, we can be insulted and choose not to take offense. God is just as free as we are either to take offense over what we do or not to take offense. If not taking offense is a good quality, then God must always choose not to take offense, since whatever good quality there is in any human being, God possesses in an infinitely greater measure.

One theological opinion is that the enormity of a sin is measured by the status of the one offended. A grave sin would have the consequence of breaking one's relationship with an infinite God. Since we are finite beings, we would be incapable of atoning for an offense against an infinite God or restoring our relationship with an infinite God.

However, to measure a crime by the status of the one offended is patently false. It is far worse to murder a child than to steal from a millionaire. The gravity of our wrongful acts depends not upon the one offended, but upon the damage caused. Furthermore, there is no way we can cause harm to God. We are finite creatures, and as such incapable of doing any act so evil that it would have infinite consequences. Theologians may be correct in saying that as finite beings we are unable to atone for an infinite offense, but they fail to understand that we are unable to create an infinite evil in the first place.

The absence of infinite offenses and infinite consequences rules out the possibility of eternal punishment. Does it rule out the possibility that sin can result in suffering?

Human Suffering

We cannot blame a loving God for human suffering, but God can allow suffering without causing it. Why God allows specific tragedies and disasters we cannot explain fully. In part, though, we can say that God respects our freedom, just as much as parents respect the freedom of their adult children. We have the freedom to injure ourselves, and others can abuse their freedom to injure us. Another explanation is that the challenges we face offer us an opportunity grow in love.

And while God does not punish those who sin, God can let us *reap what we sow*. Ruling out eternal punishment does not prevent us from freely refusing to love and to enjoy the love that God offers us — for who knows how long.

> Do not be deceived. God cannot be mocked. What a person sows that they will reap. (Galatians 6:7, OEB)

If, for example, we would in some way experience the sufferings we have inflicted on others, this could be a path to grow more in love, since all our experiences, both pleasurable and painful, can and should be used as a way to grow in love. To let us reap what we sow is to let us experience the law of cause and effect, without meaning that God retaliates and punishes us.

So what about suffering and punishment for sin? God *seeks neither revenge nor punishment, but the law of cause and effect determines that all our actions have consequences.* To reap what we sow does not mean that whenever we suffer it is because of some sin we have committed. We live in a world where suffering can happen for many reasons. All our experiences, both pleasurable and painful, are to be used as ways to grow in love.

How God looks upon sinners becomes clearer if we examine how a parent can look upon a son or daughter guilty of a serious crime. A good parent would never approve of that child's action, but would continue to look on erring children with love regardless of the wrongdoing. Such a parent would keep on seeing one's child as lovable; and God, as perfect love, does the same. God sees us as lovable, because we are lovable and always remain God's children.

Justice and Punishment

What about punishment for crime? Doesn't justice demand that criminals make restitution and pay their debt to society for harm done?

The oldest and perhaps best known legal code comes from the Mesopotamian King Hammurabi, who ruled Babylon from 1792 to 1750 BCE. His code initiated the *lex talionis,* the law making punishment fit the crime; it is often expressed by "an eye for an eye." History reveals that this law did not apply to Babylonians of every economic and social status equally. The wealthy, the poor, and those in between were treated differently. But generally, the code applied reciprocity for crimes: to cause a death would result in being put to death.

The code of Hammurabi found its way into Hebrew law after the Israelites left Egypt:

> "But if any harm follows, then you must take life for life, eye for eye, tooth for tooth, hand for hand, foot for foot, burning for burning, wound for wound, and bruise for bruise." (Exodus 21:23-24, NHEB)

This law of reciprocity, of making one pay in kind for damage done, was deemed unsatisfactory by Jesus:

> "You have heard that it was said — 'An eye for an eye and a tooth for a tooth.' But I say to you that you must not resist those who wrong you; but, if anyone strikes you on the right cheek, turn the other to them also." (Matthew 5:38-39, OEB)

He rejected the traditional norms and designated new rules:

> "If someone sues you for your shirt, let them have your cloak as well. If you are forced to carry a soldier's pack for one mile, carry it two. Give to anyone who asks and, if someone wants to borrow from you, do not turn them away." (Matthew 5:40-42, OEB)

The law of "an eye for an eye" that Jesus renounced was not just a norm for individual behavior, but the civil law of the nation of Israel. He demanded a radical change in the behavior of nations and governments as well as of his individual followers.

It is unreasonable to assert that civil society cannot pass laws to protect its citizens and keep dangerous criminals from harming others. Jesus's words, then, can only be interpreted to do away with punishment for the sake of punishment. If criminals suffer imprisonment or deprivation of any kind, the purpose allowed under Jesus's norms would be rehabilitation or help in growing in love of others. To love and forgive our enemies constitute the path to follow for nations and governments, as well as for individuals.

The image of an all-loving God cannot be reconciled with an image of a vindictive God dishing out punishment. Punishment is something we bring upon ourselves as a result of our actions and intentions. All our thoughts and actions have consequences, good or bad.

We reap the consequences of our actions in this life or in the next.

Cause and Effect

Although we can look upon offenses as a debt always to be forgiven, we must also view crimes as incurring a debt that must still be atoned for by the offender. The law of cause and effect — that we reap what we sow — determines that when we cause harm, we incur an obligation to repair the resulting damage. It is true that God forgives us, and others may forgive us as well; nevertheless, we sow a debt we must reap.

God's love and forgiveness and the law of cause and effect both stand together. Even when forgiven, we must always repair any harm we cause, whether in this life or hereafter.

Further comments will be made on this topic in the sections on *giving thanks* and *loving by acting.*

Hell

If we, as finite beings, are incapable of causing an infinite injustice or inducing limitless suffering, then what about the often preached warnings about the eternal flames of hell?

Although we have concluded that God never takes offense, always forgives, and never seeks revenge, there are a number of reasons not to smugly imagine that we can drift through life doing whatever we please without suffering any consequences:

1. God respects our free will. Affirming the axiom that our purpose in this life and in the next is to attain unconditional love, we affirm that God will never force us to love, either now or in eternity. When we die, we still

have the freedom to choose love or not. If we have become so habituated and stubborn in this life as to refuse to love, there is no reason to think that we will change at the time of death. In other words, our free will makes us capable of creating our own hell.

2. Although near-death experiences are not proof of what happens to us when we die, their consistent, though anecdotal, testimony deserves serious consideration. One of the most frequently reported experiences is the past-life review, in which a person experiences all the sufferings that one has inflicted on anyone else during this lifetime. The past-life review is often cited by near-death experiencers as the primary motive for changing the way they had been living.

3. All our actions have consequences: "We reap what we sow" is the law of cause and effect. And if we inflict severe harm on others, we cannot rule out reaping severe corrections, even if not for eternity. Even if hell or suffering the consequences of our actions is not eternal, some actions are so horrific that they can impact thousands — if not millions — of people with repercussions that can ripple through eons. We are incapable of defining — or even imagining — the extent of the sufferings we can bring upon ourselves.

A word of caution: It is tempting to think of those guilty of the most heinous crimes as enduring torments in hell. Jesus warned us,

> "Do not judge and you will not be judged. For, just as you judge others, you will yourselves be judged, and the standard that you use will be used for you." (Matthew 7:1-2, OEB)

9

The Spiritual Practice of Forgiving

The spiritual practice of *forgiving* is, like *perceiving*, based on the Lord's Prayer, "Forgive us our trespasses as we forgive those who trespass against us." When you say this prayer, say it slowly and meditate on each petition, especially in asking for forgiveness. In forgiving, you are truly forgiven.

There are two other passages fundamental to this practice: (1) Matthew 18:21-35, the parable of the unjust servant (steward) and (2) Luke 7:36-50, the story of the woman who anointed Jesus's feet. Read these passages and take time to reflect on them.

Remember these principles: (1) God always forgives. This is the same as saying that God never takes offense, no matter what the crime may be. (2) The only way to block the benefit of God's forgiveness is to refuse to forgive others. (3) Therefore, we must forgive everyone who offends or hurts us, and we must do so over and over again.

We are not *reservoirs* of God's love and forgiveness. We are *channels*.

Forgiving is not a one-time action, but a *practice* to be repeated constantly. Some find this practice difficult, so here are some suggestions to make it easier:

First, learn to love and forgive yourself. God always forgives you, even before you ask. Learn to acknowledge the gift, not just with regret, but with love and gratitude, and by forgiving others.

Second, do not confuse forgiving with suffering abuse. If you are in an abusive situation, get out of it as soon as you can. Never let yourself become a victim of any kind of abuse — verbal, mental or physical. To do so is not a virtue and never helps you or anyone else.

Third, you may find it hard to forgive certain people or offenses. If so, admit the difficulty, but do not think that something is wrong with you. Change the way you approach this practice.

It is often the small things that hinder us from growing spiritually rather than the big things. If you want to run a marathon, you do not start by running twenty-five miles the first day. First you run around the block, then you run a mile, then five miles, and you keep on running farther and farther. Forgiveness takes practice; learn by starting off small, but be consistent. Start working on forgiving small slights and offenses, such as when people ignore you, cut you off in traffic, or step in front of you in the grocery line. Practice in forgiving small things makes it easier to forgive big things.

When you leave this life, you leave everything behind except your relationships. When someone hurts you, whether in a big way or a small way, that relationship is damaged; and it is as though both of you are chained to each other. This chain does not automatically go away over time. Anger and resentment will only make the chain heavier and more painful. But you have the power to forgive, and when you use the power to forgive, you break the chain.

When *forgiving* is difficult, be sure that you are still practicing *perceiving*. Unless you can see that those you need to forgive are lovable in God's eyes — that is, unless you can see that God also forgives your enemies — you will find *forgiving* impossible. To forgive is to love, and you cannot love someone unless you see that person as lovable.

If you need to apologize, apologize for what you have done and not for who you are. Admitting wrongdoing does not mean you are no longer a lovable child of God.

Do not worry about being forgiven. You have already received forgiveness in abundance. Forgiveness is not the gift you need to *receive*. It is *the gift you need to give.*

Reflect on Jesus's words in Luke's passion narrative. From the cross, Jesus said,

> Then Jesus said, "Father, forgive them; they do not know what they are doing." (Luke 23:34, OEB)[30]

He did not pray that his persecutors would repent and be sorry. He did not pray that they would change their ways and end the crucifixion. He did not pray that they atone for their crime. He prayed only that they be forgiven. He gave forgiveness as a gift, not as something that his persecutors could earn.

---

[30]Some manuscripts omit this passage.

Your Notebook

Here are a few suggestions on notes to put into the first quarter of each page of your notebook: Write down the name (disguised, if you wish) of someone who has caused you harm or any kind of inconvenience. If you are just beginning your notebook, it may be easier to first name those who have been responsible for small injuries rather than major ones.

List possible reasons or factors that led the offender to wrongful actions — for example, one's upbringing, education, possibly having been abused in childhood, or making an erroneous judgment because of not knowing the facts.

List the good actions or qualities of that person — that is, one's redeeming features. Put down ways in which that person might be making up for the wrong done to you.

Formula for Forgiveness

Jesus began, "There were two people who were in debt to a moneylender; one owed five hundred silver coins, and the other fifty. As they were unable to pay, he forgave them both. Which of them, do you think, will love him the more?"

"I suppose," answered Simon, "it will be the man to whom he forgave the greater debt."

"You are right," said Jesus, and then, turning to the woman, he said to Simon, "Do you see this woman? I came into your house — you gave me no water for my feet, but she has made my feet wet with her tears and dried them with her hair. You did not give me one kiss, but she, from the moment I came in, has not ceased to kiss my feet. You did not anoint even my head with oil, but she has anointed my feet with perfume. So I tell you, her great love shows that her sins, many as they are, have been pardoned. One who is pardoned little loves little." Then he said to the woman,

> "Your sins have been pardoned." The other
> guests began to say to one another, "Who is this
> man who even pardons sins?" But Jesus said to
> the woman, "Your faith has delivered you; go, and
> peace be with you." (Luke 7:40-50, OEB)

The following poem is based on Luke 7:36-50. Jesus is invited to eat at a Pharisee's home, and a woman known as a sinner anoints Jesus's feet with ointment. The Pharisee questions Jesus, who in turn tells a parable in which two persons in are debt, one for five hundred denarii and the other for fifty. Both debts are forgiven, and Jesus asks which debtor will love the creditor more.

The Pharisee, Simon, thinks it would be the one released from the bigger debt.

For Jesus, the answer is correct. Then he rebukes Simon for not treating him as well as the woman did. He says that she shows much love, because her many sins have been forgiven. This is not what we expect: Jesus states that she loves much because she has been forgiven much, and not that she has been forgiven because of her love. Then he tells the woman to go in peace.

Our faith is a mosaic or a picture or a platter
filled with morsels that taste good with every bite.
To be forgiven and to love are the things that really matter,
and it's essential that we get their order right.

For our faith does not begin with a dogma or a creed,
but acceptance of forgiveness for each crime.
Forgiveness for our sins, and not belief, is what we need,
and our love will follow later in due time.

When much has been forgiven, then much love will later
    follow.
If less forgiven, then our love will be less, too.
To reverse the order here will make a faith that's dead and
    hollow,
since forgiveness cannot to our love be due.

The reign of God is like a banquet, like a feast we're called
    to eat
on finest china with a knife and fork of gold.
When sin creeps in, it spills the cream and sours the wine
    and spoils the meat,
and rots the fruit, and coats the cake and bread with mold

When food's destroyed and famine's come, we die with
    hunger through the night.
Our tongue is parched, our mouth is dry, and burning pain
    keeps us awake.
To hide our shame we force a smile and let no other know
    our plight—
for dignity and for our pride, and for our ego's sake.

What mother, when she knows her child would like a loaf
    of bread,
instead would offer on a plate a decorated stone?
And if a child would like a fish, what father would instead
throw her a scorpion, then leave her all alone?

When we by sin our dinner spoil, what action does God
    take?
Should we refuse to eat our food, does God send us away?
Unlike our parents here on earth, no threats does our God
    make.
Instead, a bigger banquet is prepared; forgiveness is God's
    way.

Always does our God forgive, forgiveness ne'er
    withholding.
No condition need we meet, the gift is always there.
God is like a mother hen, always us enfolding
in her wings forgivingly, to keep us in her care.

To the banquet of forgiveness do not come with empty
    hands.
Bring your host and hostess a small gift that you can share.
A small gift of your thanksgiving is what etiquette
    demands.
Not quantity, but quality, will show you really care.

As for your selection, there's no doubt that you will
    question
how to find a proper gift that you could bring.
To solve this old dilemma there is offered this suggestion:
a gift of your best oil will top any other thing.

Bring extra virgin olive oil, the finest you can find.
Use it on your salad or as marinade for meat.
If none's for sale, and out of time, you see you're in a bind,
a walnut oil will also do to make the meal complete.

Essential oils are finer yet — try frankincense and myrrh.
Just put a drop upon your wrist and rub it on your skin.
There's also oil of lemongrass, of chamomile, and fir,
and oil of sage, and oil of rose, and oil of mandarin.

Take oils of lavender and lime and splash them in your
    hair.
And just before the meal is served and all sit down to eat,
please let their soft aroma fill and saturate the air,
and take more oil and with your hair go wipe the Teacher's
    feet.

The reign of God is like a banquet, like a feast we're called
to eat.
The feast is pardon granted to us, now already it is ours.
Accepting love is love returning, life with pardon now
replete.
More accepted, more returned, for those forgiven God
empowers.

Faith that saves is love in action, love responding to God's
call.
Receiving pardon for our failures is a treasure our heart
craves.
By returning love for pardon, we in spirit have it all.
Displaying love when we're forgiven, Jesus calls the faith
that saves.

Part III

Blessing

10

The Spoken Word

in the Old Testament

Isaac and the Blessing of Jacob

When Isaac, the son of Abraham, lay dying, he had to designate which of his twin sons, Esau or Jacob, would be the
one to become the father of God's chosen people.[31] Since
Esau was the older as well as his favorite, Isaac intended
to designate him his chief heir. Confined to his bed, he
could no longer see. He called Esau and asked him to go
hunt for game and prepare it for him as he liked, so that
he could bless him and confirm him as his heir.

Rebekah, Isaac's wife, overheard the conversation. For her, Jacob was the favorite, and so she had him

---

[31] Genesis 27.

prepare food for his father and dress in animal skins so that his arms would feel like the hairy arms of Esau. When Jacob went into his father's tent, his voice could not be changed, but Isaac felt his arms and believed that he was with Esau. He then gave Jacob his blessing, saying that his son would rule over his brothers and over nations.

Later Esau came to his father and asked for his blessing. Isaac was dismayed. He had been deceived into making Jacob the father of God's chosen people. Being too late, Esau had to settle for a lesser blessing.

When Isaac realized that he had given his blessing to the wrong son, why didn't he just say, "Oh, I made a mistake. I'll just take that blessing back and give it to you, Esau," instead?

The reason is that the Hebrews believed that our spoken word, once pronounced, continued on. The spoken word had its own existence, and there was no way to take it back. A word once spoken had a life of its own. Its power continued on, so that the power of the word always existed to produce its effect.

The Spoken Word

We see a similar idea in Genesis and elsewhere in the Bible. God says, "Let there be light," and there was light. God's spoken word had the power to create whatever the word meant. Our power to speak is a way in which we share God's power to create.

The biblical image of a blessing is based on the irreversible power of the spoken word. It is more than a prayer. We say what we *intend* to happen, and speaking our intention *makes* it happen.

11

The Spoken Word in the Gospels

Jesus and the Power to Bless

In the first century CE, belief in the power of the spoken word was still alive. After King Herod imprisoned John the Baptist, his fear of the prophet's powers kept him from putting John to death. His indecisive attitude took an unexpected turn when he put on a birthday party for himself and was entranced by the dancing of his daughter Herodias. He promised to give her whatever she asked, even half his kingdom. Her mother told her to ask for the head of John the Baptist. Because he had sworn an oath before his guests, he at once had John beheaded, and his head was brought to the king. Herod gave his word, which could not be retracted.[32]

The power of Jesus's word is evident in the story of the Roman centurion:

> After Jesus had entered Capernaum, a captain in the Roman army came up to him, entreating his help. "Sir," he said, "my manservant is lying ill at my house with a stroke of paralysis, and is suffering terribly."
>
> "I will come and cure him," answered Jesus. "Sir," the captain went on, "I am unworthy to receive you under my roof; but only speak, and my manservant will be cured. For I myself am a man under the orders of others, with soldiers under me; and, if I say to one of them 'Go,' he goes, and to another 'Come,' he comes, and to my slave 'Do this,' he does it."
>
> Jesus was surprised to hear this, and said to those who were following him, "Never I tell you, in any Israelite have I met with such faith as this! Yes, and many will come in from East and West and take their places beside Abraham, Isaac, and Jacob, in the kingdom of heaven; while the heirs to the kingdom will be banished into the darkness outside; there, there will be weeping and grinding of teeth." Then Jesus said to the captain, "Go now, and it will be according to your faith." And the man was cured that very hour. (Matthew 8:5-13, OEB)[33]

The spoken word was supposed to have power for the patriarchs and for Jesus, but what about us? Is the spoken word powerful in itself or because of the one who speaks? In the Sermon on the Mount, Jesus gave this command:

---

[32] Mark 6:17-29.
[33] See also Luke 7:1-10.

> "But to you who hear I say — love your enemies, show kindness to those who hate you, bless those who curse you, pray for those who insult you." (Luke 6:27-28, OEB)

To obey his command we must have the power to bless. Keep in mind that Jesus's words were directed to the Galileans and to the people of his time and not to a select few. Jesus expected everyone to bless one's enemies. The power to bless is innate in every child of God. In words that echo Jesus's command, the apostle Paul tells the Romans, "Bless your persecutors — bless and never curse."[34]

The Power of a Blessing

The original meaning of a blessing is the English synonym, *benediction*, which comes from the Latin *benedicere*, with the etymological meaning of "to say well or to say something good." Since words were seen as continuing to exert their power long after being spoken, to bless has the connotation of saying something good with the power to effect the intent of the spoken word. Similarly, to curse means to harm someone with evil words or intent.

In our time the notion of words having power is not widespread. However, people today do occasionally think of a curse as having some kind of evil power, such as "being under a curse." A curse is thought of as an evil spell, while a blessing seems to be a prayer.

While a curse might be considered to be an evil spell by anyone, especially someone with demonic power, a benediction or blessing is more often than not

---

[34] Romans 12:14, OEB. See also First Corinthians 4:12 and First Peter 3:9.

considered to be a prayer offered by a cleric, usually or-dained in an organized religion. Priests and ministers bless water, animals, cars, and religious objects; and their laity may look upon these objects as somehow made different. On the other hand, the power to bless is perceived as a power possessed solely by those in a reli-gious hierarchy.

Over the centuries the followers of Jesus have for-gotten the power of their own spoken word and allowed the power to bless to be wrought solely by their clergy. The power to bless is not something we have lost, but something we have given away.

Blessing as a Universal Power

Because the power to bless is practiced almost exclu-sively by priests, ministers and other clergy, two ques-tions arise: First, did Jesus ever give any special powers to his disciples: The answer is, yes, he did. The one time we know of is in the ninth chapter of Luke, when Jesus gave his disciples the power to heal and to cast out de-mons. These powers may have been one and the same, since it was believed that sickness was caused by demons or evil spirits.

At the end of chapter nine, the disciples returned to Jesus:

> John said, "Sir, we saw a man driving out demons by using your name, and we tried to prevent him, because he does not follow you with us."
>
> "None of you must prevent him," Jesus said to John; "whoever's not against you is for you." (Luke 9:49-50, OEB)

So the answer to the first question is yes, Jesus at least on one occasion gave his disciples special power; that power, however, was not exclusive to them.

The second question is, did the disciples pass on their privileged power to their successors? This question is not a matter of dogma, but of history.

History does not tell us all that the apostles did after the resurrection, but we do have reliable information about the activities of Paul, who established communities throughout the empire. Paul's first letter to the Corinthians, for example, tells us that the Corinthians celebrated a Last Supper ritual, but that in doing so they ate their full while letting the poor go hungry; the community was in chaos.[35]

Paul wrote his epistle to reprimand and correct the people of Corinth, and his letter is addressed not to anyone in charge, but to the entire community. If someone had been appointed to lead the community in his absence, he would have addressed that person; but he did not. He did not write to an appointed leader, because there was none. And there was no reason for Paul to appoint successors in any of the communities he founded, since he believed that Jesus was going to return during his lifetime.

The answer to the second question is, if we rely on the only record of apostolic authority, which is that of Paul, then no, there were no successors to receive privileged powers from the apostles, not even in celebrating the Last Supper ritual.

The power to bless was never an exclusive privilege of the apostles or of a later hierarchy. Both Jesus and Paul commanded everyone to bless their enemies.

---

[35] 1 Corinthians 11.

The Power of Intention

An examination of the nonlocal power of human intention has not evaded the scientific community. Dr. Larry Dossey discusses "experiments, which seem clearly to show that mental activity can be used to influence people nonlocally, at a distance, without their knowledge." He warns "that prayer can be used at a distance to *harm* people without their knowledge."[36]

In all the experiments concerning the effects of prayer, there has been no discernible difference based on the faith or belief systems of those involved. *Blessing*, like *forgiving*, is a power inherent in our nature as God's children.

---

[36] Larry Dossey, M.D., *Healing Words: The Power of Prayer and the Practice of Medicine,* HarperSanFrancisco, 1993, page 79.

12

The Spiritual Practice of Blessing

The power in the practice of *blessing* is not magic, but comes from God and the divine power you possess as a child of God. It is essential to believe you have this power as well as truly intend to bless. To strengthen your intention, devices like these are helpful: (1) gestures, such as raising your hands over the object or person being blessed or laying your hands on a sick person; (2) the use of signs, such as the sign of a cross over a person or object, sprinkling water, or anointing with oil; (3) playing music or singing an inspirational song; (4) lighting candles or incense; (5) joining with others, as by standing in a circle, by joining hands, by taking turns in praying, and the like; (6) using religious objects, such as crucifixes, images, or statues, which are appropriate to your culture.

You can start with the common practice of blessing your food before meals. Make this a short time of prayer in which you intend the food you are about to eat to benefit both your physical and spiritual health.

If you are a parent, bless your children, perhaps before they go to bed; and you can also bless you spouse. From time to time you can bless your home, your garden (especially when you are planting), or your car (perhaps when it is new or before taking a trip).

Keep in mind the purpose of a blessing, which is so that someone may receive God's love, strength, peace or consolation, or some kind of divine healing, either physical or spiritual. Since a blessing is a spiritual action, it is intended to connect one with the divine. Whoever receives a blessing is directed to be made holier or brought closer to God in some way. Objects are blessed with the intention of asking divine or angelic guidance for those who use them.

In giving a blessing, we first intend that what we are asking for be of spiritual benefit to others and to ourselves. Although we give a blessing, a sick person may not get well, crops may still wither, and a car accident may happen. We are unable to judge the spiritual benefit of a blessing.

Blessings are not substitutes for seeing a physician, taking medication, driving safely, doing an act of charity (such as helping a homeless person), or other common sense actions.

Jesus specifically requires that we bless our enemies. This kind of blessing is difficult for some. It requires two basic elements: (1) a sincere prayer for the other person, and (2) a firm intention that you want something good for that person. If you find this difficult because of an injury you have endured, ask for help from God or your angels to offer your prayer. It is essential that you are building on the first two spiritual practices of *perceiving* and *forgiving,* so that you know in your heart that your offender is your sister or brother and a child of God like you, and that you have forgiven that person.

You can practice *blessing* in your daily prayers or at any time in the day. All you need is a sincere intention. But the practice requires repetition. Like any prayer, its effectiveness is increased by doing it with others. Consider the practice of *blessing* a huge opportunity — a chance to use God's love and power to change the world for the better. You have a chance to bring peace and love to others on earth.

Keep in mind that all blessings have power, and that their power is the love you have in your heart. Also remember that a blessing is not just what you receive, but what you give, and it is what you *are.*

Your Notebook

Your list of those you wish to bless can include not only family and friends, but also those who have hurt you. Write down how you would like them to change — in behavior, health, finances, or other — and what they could do for others if they made changes in their lives.

List some specific needs of those close to you: your family, friends, neighbors, your country and your world. The fulfillment of these needs can be part of your prayer of blessing.

Write down one specific blessing for at least one person you dislike or who has harmed you. If you have a particular person in mind, write down the exact blessing you would like that person to receive.

At the same time, remind yourself that your blessing and prayer may be answered in other ways besides what you may intend.

Word

After Jesus had entered Capernaum, a captain in the Roman army came up to him, entreating his help. "Sir," he said, "my manservant is lying ill at my house with a stroke of paralysis, and is suffering terribly."

"I will come and cure him," answered Jesus.

"Sir," the captain went on, "I am unworthy to receive you under my roof; but only speak, and my manservant will be cured. For I myself am a man under the orders of others, with soldiers under me; and, if I say to one of them 'Go,' he goes, and to another 'Come,' he comes, and to my slave 'Do this,' he does it."

Jesus was surprised to hear this, and said to those who were following him, "Never I tell you, in any Israelite have I met with such faith as this! Yes, and many will come in from East and West and take their places beside Abraham, Isaac, and Jacob, in the kingdom of heaven; while the heirs to the kingdom will be banished into the darkness outside; there, there will be weeping and grinding of teeth." Then Jesus said to the captain, "Go now, and it will be according to your faith." And the man was cured that very hour. (Matthew 8:5 13 OEB)

"Truly, truly, I tell you, he who believes in me, the works that I do, he will do also; and he will do greater works than these, because I am going to the Father. (John 14:12 NHEB)

The following poem is based first on Matthew 8:5-13, the story of Jesus healing the servant of a centurion. Secondly, it relies on John 14:12-14, in which Jesus says that we will do even greater works than he has done and that our Father will do whatever we ask in Jesus's name. Thirdly, it refers to the story of Isaac blessing Jacob in Genesis 27:30-37.

A thunderstorm can blacken skies, can turn the day
to night. A single bomb, we understand, can turn
a city into dust, can make skyscrapers burn.
We know the power that sunshine has to turn the night to
    day,
but do we know the power we use in every word we say?

The words we say to children have the power to change
their lives. Such simple words as "Yes, I know you can,"
can make a child into a woman or a man.
And still the power of words to make or break is not so
    strange
as how we waste our precious power of verbal interchange.

The churches teach the power of words, and that's the
    reason why
priests bless our medals, rosaries and churches, homes and
    cars.
They bless all things from soup to nuts, from shotguns to
    guitars.
And do we know what happens on the earth or in the sky
when blessings are pronounced to holy water sanctify?

Is there a special power that some possess, a force
they have by virtue of the office that they hold,
so that an automatic wonder will unfold
whene'er the proper words of blessing those ordained
    enforce?
And others not ordained are without power in their
    discourse?

Remember Isaac, who when dying did pronounce
his final blessing to a clever, younger son —
a blessing that by lies and trickery was won —
and when his elder son in tears his presence did announce,
could not his prior word of blessing cancel or renounce.

What is the power that words possess, a force so great
that once pronounced, goes out unseen to harm, to heal,
and future generations' certain fate to seal?
Do words we say go on and on, just waiting to create
the deeds we asked them for, and now we're helpless to
    negate?

A Roman soldier knew the power a single word
possessed. "When I say, 'Go,' my servants go. When I
say, 'Come,' they come. Just say the word, I'll know that
    my
sick servant has been healed." When such deep faith the
    Teacher heard,
he said the word, and at that hour the miracle occurred.

We marvel that a single word could break the chain
of time and space. And yet, the Teacher promised we
could do the same and even greater works than he.
Whatever signs he worked on earth, we'll greater signs
    attain.
Our words have power we know not of, that no one can
    restrain.

Our words are jagged lightning flashes in the night.
Our words are peals of thunder booming in the storm.
Our words are life we give or take, make cold or warm
the hearts of those who hear. Respect the word's most
    awesome might.
It can be used for good or ill; respect it, use it right.

Part IV

Giving Thanks

13

Gratitude as a Duty

One of the first expressions parents teach their children is, "Thank you." If a child receives a gift without saying, "Thank you," parents give a gentle reminder, "Now what do you say?" The obligation to be grateful and express thanks is so much taken for granted that failure can be met with anger.

God's Gifts

Thanksgiving Day is the holiday when Americans reflect on all they have to be grateful for. On that day you may have experienced a time of reflection in which those present named a significant gift for which they were grateful. The gifts named might have been things like good health, surviving an accident, friends and family, getting a good job, and the like. This was not the attitude of the apostle Paul. When Paul recommends giving thanks, he does not list all the pleasant things that we may put at the top of our list. Instead, he says,

> Sing and make music in your hearts to the Lord. Always give thanks for everything to our God and Father, in the name of our Lord Jesus Christ. (Ephesians 5:19-20, OEB)

> Always be joyful; never cease to pray; under all circumstances give thanks to God. For this is his will for you as made known in Christ Jesus. (1 Thessalonians 5:16-18, OEB)

Paul asks us to be grateful not just when everything goes well, but also when misfortune crosses our path. He expects us to see good in all things, including what appears as harmful.

Being grateful means looking beyond appearances and seeing good everywhere in whatever we endure.

Universal Indebtedness

For many, there is a special debt of gratitude to one individual (a teacher, a coach, or a friend) or to a traumatic event (an accident, a near-death experience, or a dramatic recovery from illness) that changed one's life. Such markers in one's life stand out as reminders of one's debt of gratitude. Easier to overlook, however, are the multitude of gifts from those we have never met, strangers whose names may be unknown, some living, some long deceased.

From the moment we took our first breath, we depended on others for everything we were to have and were to become. Our civilization and culture were formed by countless inventors, scientists, teachers, farmers, physicians, politicians, construction workers, soldiers, and others. We cannot live as we do without all those not only in our own community, but those who are sources of food, clothing, and knowledge in countries across the globe. We are dependent on millions everywhere in the world.

There is no such thing as a self-made human being. No matter how hard one has worked to achieve awards, build a career, accumulate wealth, or raise a family, nothing could have been accomplished without help from others, including civilization itself. We are all dependent upon each other, and we owe a debt of gratitude for the benefits we have received from others everywhere — gifts we must not take for granted.

Expressions of Gratitude

The parable of the unjust steward,[37] in which Jesus taught the lesson of forgiveness, is also an implicit example of how to show gratitude. Although shown mercy for a large debt, the steward did not show mercy for a small one. The lesson of showing mercy or granting forgiveness is an example of a universal principle: we best express our gratitude for the gifts we have received by sharing those gifts with others.

The cycle of life determines that we naturally pass on to others what we have received: we receive life from our parents, and we pass it on to our children. And that sharing of life includes the gifts of wealth, education, moral values, and opportunities.

When invited for dinner, it is common to reciprocate by giving an invitation in return. Otherwise, a verbal or written thank you is expected as a common courtesy.

---

[37] Matthew 18:23-35.

Gratitude makes us more human and unites us with our sisters and brothers as children in God's family.

The Ten Lepers

We have in the Gospels few explicit commands to give thanks; but in the story of the cure of ten lepers, Jesus told how he felt when gratitude was lacking:

> On the way to Jerusalem Jesus passed between Samaria and Galilee. As he was entering a village, ten lepers met him. Standing still, some distance off, they called out loudly, "Jesus! Sir! Pity us!"
>
> When Jesus saw them, he said, "Go and show yourselves to the priest."
>
> And, as they were on their way, they were made clean. One of them, finding he was cured, came back, praising God loudly, and threw himself on his face at Jesus's feet, thanking him for what he had done; and this man was a Samaritan.
> "Were not all the ten made clean?" exclaimed Jesus. "But the nine — where are they? Were there none to come back and praise God except this foreigner? Get up," he said to him, "and go on your way. Your faith has delivered you." (Luke 17:11-19, OEB)

What Jesus expected on that occasion is what we always expect of others and what others always expect of us: to be grateful for every gift received and to express our gratitude with thanks.

14

The Spiritual Practice of

Giving Thanks

If we see ourselves as God's children and acknowledge the gift of God's forgiveness, then *giving thanks* should come naturally. Like the first three practices, *giving thanks* has to be regularly repeated. It can be done at any time, but to make it a permanent way of thinking, do it on a regular schedule, such as after meals or as part of other prayers or meditation.

Besides thanking God for all we have and are, another ingredient is required, which is to express our gratitude to others. Besides saying "Thank you" or sending "thank you" notes, we need to be generous in returning acts of kindness.

Be grateful to those who have given you a "second chance" when you needed it for any reason. Befriend those who have helped you, at least by passing on the gift to others and by blessing your benefactors.

Being grateful in hard times becomes easier by making a practice of *giving thanks* frequently for the small gifts of life. Like *forgiving*, we find it easier to face the big challenges if we practice *giving thanks* often for small gifts.

Your Notebook

To make *giving thanks* a habit, write down in the evening one event that happened during the day for which you are grateful. Think of commonplace happenings, such as someone holding the door open for you or a motorist stopping to let you go through a crosswalk. Maybe someone found an item you lost, or you may have been served your favorite dish for dinner. Reflect on these events and offer a prayer of blessing for your benefactors.

Write down any blessings that come to mind: having good friends, enjoying good health, pleasant weather, or just the gift of life.

Poor self-esteem can block your efforts to be a loving person and to put your good intentions into practice. Negative criticism, misfortune, and occasional lack of success reinforce a negative self-image. Since negative images are much more forceful than positive, block out strong negative images with even more powerful, positive ones. Frequently review the successes in your life. Make yourself aware of your talents and abilities by writing down in your notebook even your smallest accomplishments, such as making friends, forgiving others, raising a family, learning something new (anything from how to boil an egg to learning a new language), helping others, making a contribution to a just cause, or holding your tongue when someone makes you angry.

Your successes are true blessings. Be aware of how others helped you to succeed, and give thanks. An honest assessment of your talents will help you to undertake goals that may otherwise seem beyond your reach.

A Psalm of Thanksgiving

Learn to be merciful — even as your Father is merciful. Do not judge, and you will not be judged; do not condemn, and you will not be condemned. Forgive, and you will be forgiven. (Luke 6:36-37 OEB)

Give thanks to the LORD for his goodness:
for his kindness endures forever. (Psalm 136:1 OEB)

Seek to be filled with the Spirit of God, and speak to one another in psalms and hymns and sacred songs. Sing and make music in your hearts to the Lord. Always give thanks for everything to our God and Father, in the name of our Lord Jesus Christ. (Ephesians 5:18-20 OEB)

Give thanks to God, for God is good; God's love will never
    end.
Our God is Father, Mother, too, an everlasting friend.

I thank you, God, for all that is, for all that was, for all
that will be, too. I thank you for the sun and rain, for skies
both gray and clear. I thank you for the summertime, for
    fall
and winter cold, and for the spring when dead to new life
    rise.

Give thanks to God, for God is good; God's love will never
    end.
Our God is Father, Mother, too, an everlasting friend.

I thank you for the gifts I see, for those that I see not.
Is what I see the best for me, or what is hid from view?
For trees to send their branches deep into the heavens, what
they need much more are even deeper roots, that earth sink
    through.

Give thanks to God, for God is good; God's love will never
    end.
Our God is Father, Mother, too, an everlasting friend.

If I should praise God for the day, then truly should
I praise God for the night. I must not judge between the
    two,
for both do need each other, just as in the night we would
not see the stars, did not the darkness light pursue.

Give thanks to God, for God is good; God's love will never
    end.
Our God is Father, Mother, too, an everlasting friend.

Astronomers do scan the skies; their telescopes they point
to capture signals from the universe beyond. But light
is not all that they see. Their pictures do not disappoint,
revealing x-rays, microwaves, and visions out of sight.

Give thanks to God, for God is good; God's love will never
    end.
Our God is Father, Mother, too, an everlasting friend.

Is darkness but the light I cannot see? How can I stand
in judgment of the darkness to condemn the light outside
the narrow spectrum I can see? O God, I thank you and
I praise you in the light and darkness where you do abide.

Give thanks to God, for God is good; God's love will never
    end.
Our God is Father, Mother, too, an everlasting friend.

I thank you, God, for life just as it is, and not as I
would have it be. How can I be so sure that what I do
perceive as evil is not but a blessing that my eye
can't see? I thank you for the good and evil, too.

Give thanks to God, for God is good; God's love will never
    end.
Our God is Father, Mother, too, an everlasting friend.

The world is made of black and white, of ev'ry shade of
    gray,
of rainbow's hues displayed in souls of all throughout the
    earth.
I thank you, we are one with you, and one with all who
    may
return to us, God's children all, sent here from death to
    birth.

Give thanks to God, for God is good; God's love will never
    end.
Our God is Father, Mother, too, an everlasting friend.

Part V

Praying

15

Jesus's Teaching about Prayer

Spiritual directors, religious instructors and churches teach a wide variety of oral prayers and methods of praying: meditation, centering prayer, breathing methods, prayers that vary with the time of year or time of day, weekly and daily worship services, and prayers that specify one's posture, such as standing, sitting or kneeling.

Jesus taught only one prayer, the Lord's Prayer.

Typical church teaching lists four categories of prayer: (1) worship, praise or adoration; (2) sorrow or repentance; (3) thanksgiving; and (4) petition. Further distinctions are made depending on whether one prays alone or with others, whether one prays for others or for oneself, and so on.

Jesus's instructions on prayer apply almost exclusively to prayers of petition. For example:

"Ask, and it will be given to you; search, and you will find; knock, and the door will be opened to you. For the person who asks receives, the person who searches finds, and to the door will be opened to the person who knocks. Who among you, when their child asks them for bread, will give them a stone, or when they ask for a fish, will give them a snake? If you, then, wicked though you are, know how to give good gifts to your children, how much more will your Father who is in heaven give what is good to those who ask him!" (Matthew 7:7-11, OEB)

Jesus tells us to bless our enemies; this, too, is a form of petition. Notably absent from his teachings is any reference to the need to offer prayers of worship or adoration. On the other hand, Jesus's words about the prayer of petition are phrased as a command. In the next chapter we will discuss the why and how of the prayer of petition.

16

The Essence of Asking

The Need to Ask in Prayer

The first spiritual practice of *perceiving* reminds us that we are all interconnected as God's children and are one with the universe. Quantum physics has illustrated the physical effects of this unity, demonstrating that we cannot conduct an experiment without being a part of that experiment. The consequence of this is that just by observing an experiment we influence the outcome. Outside the quantum level, the interconnectedness of all reality operates under the same laws, even if causes and effects are not always quite as visible. Whatever we do has an effect on the world around us. Just by observing what goes on, we influence the outcome.

With the gift of free will we can choose which of many possible futures become reality. The future is composed of many paths which have not yet come to pass. Humanity has taken many paths leading to destruction and suffering. Our purpose in life is to take a better path, to make peace, joy, and unconditional love our ultimate accomplishment. The path toward this goal, however, is not automatically achieved by humankind, since God allows us to choose alternate paths and futures.

Prayer is one of the most effective means to turn our choices into reality. The purpose of prayer is succinctly stated in the words of Gregg Braden, "Prayer...is, to us, as water is to the seed of a plant."[38]

How Prayer Works

There is no magic prayer formula to get what you want. Nor are there any unique rites or ceremonies to attain the noblest of aims, be they world peace, end to hunger, good health, or rain in the midst of drought. What our words and rituals can do, though, is to change us, so that our intention may produce an appropriate effect. How prayer works has been well described by Gregg Braden, whose explanation is summarized here.[39]

Braden enumerates three components in prayer: thought, emotion and feeling. Thought guides our emotions, but has little energy. Emotion gives energy. Feeling unites thought and emotion. For Braden, feeling is the central component of prayer.

In our prayers we say that we are *asking* for something. Often that is something we lack or believe we need,

---

[38] Gregg Braden, *The Isaiah Effect, Decoding the Lost Science of Prayer and Prophecy,* Harmony Books, New York, 2000, page 181.
[39] *Ibid.,* pages 145-181.

such as money, health, good weather, or peace. If we focus on our lack or need, our energy is misdirected away from what we want. Our prayer then becomes self-defeating.

The remedy, according to Braden, is found in feeling. If we seek peace, we need to *feel* peace. We need to intend it with our thoughts and put energy into with our emotions; but most of all we need to experience the feeling of peace within and outside ourselves. Our feeling of peace is what centers our thoughts and emotions on the positive goal of peace and away from the negative aspects of war and lack of harmony.

Another researcher, Dr. Larry Dossey, distinguishes between these two kinds of prayer: (1) directed prayer, in which we ask for a specific result, such as to be healed from cancer, and (2) nondirected prayer, which is open-ended, without a specific outcome in mind. In referring to the experiments of the Spendthrift organization of Salem, Oregon, he says that *"the most important discovery of the Spendthrift tests is that prayer works and that both methods are effective.* But in these tests the *non-*directed technique appeared quantitatively more effective, frequently yielding results that were twice as great, or more, when compared to the direct approach." [40]

As noted earlier, those who have conducted scientific studies of the effects of prayer have found that the belief system of the participants is irrelevant. *Praying,* like *blessing* and *forgiving,* is a power derived from our nature as children of God.

Begin your prayer with gratitude for all that is. Concentrate on feeling what you want to experience, and

[40] Larry Dossey, M.D., *Healing Words: The Power of Prayer and the Practice of Medicine,* HarperSanFrancisco, 1993, page 97.

conclude with gratitude "for the *opportunity* to choose which creation"[41] you experience.

---

[41] Gregg Braden, *The Isaiah Effect, Decoding the Lost Science of Prayer and Prophecy,* Harmony Books, New York, 2000, page 167. Italics are those of Gregg Braden.

17

Jesus as the Model for Prayer

As a practicing Jew, Jesus would have observed the Jewish feast days with their rituals and said the prayers common to the Jewish religion. Beyond that, the Gospels do relate times when Jesus prayed:

1. He began his ministry by spending forty days in the wilderness.[42]

2. He blessed children.[43]

3. Before his crucifixion, he prayed in the Garden of Gethsemane.

> Presently they came to a garden known as Gethsemane, and Jesus said to his disciples "Sit down here while I pray." He took with him Peter, James,

---

[42] Mark 1:12-13; Matthew 4:1-11; Luke 7:1-13.
[43] Mark 10:13-16; Matthew 19:13-15; Luke 18:15-17.

and John; and began to show signs of great dismay and deep distress of mind. "I am sad at heart," he said, "sad even to death; wait here, and watch." Going on a little further, he threw himself on the ground, and began to pray that, if it were possible, he might be spared that hour. "Abba, Father," he said, "all things are possible to you; take away this cup from me; yet, not what I will, but what you will." (Mark 14:32-36, OEB)[44]

This is a prayer of petition, with the reservation that God's will be done.

4) The Gospels give differing versions of Jesus's prayers on the cross. As a result, we cannot be certain of his words.

Of the utmost significance is how Jesus addresses God: *Abba, Father, Daddy.* His prayers were always an expression of his relationship, as a son, with God.

---

[44] See also Matthew 26:36-46 and Luke 22:39-46.

18

The Spiritual Practice of

Praying

It may be helpful to pray at specific times of the day, such as upon rising, just before retiring, or before or after meals. This is a matter of personal choice. The *Didache,* an early Christian document, recommended saying the Lord's Prayer three times a day.

Religious teachers offer many types of prayer, such as meditation or centering prayer. If you find them helpful, by all means make use of them. More important, though is to cultivate a childlike attitude in your prayers. Jesus always prayed to God as his Father, and *his attitude* is the model for our prayer more than specific prayer methods.

Instead of using your notebook for the practice of *praying*, be faithful in the other spiritual practices already discussed, and let your prayers come naturally from these practices. Any notes you wish to make about *praying* can be combined with those on *blessing.*

If some cautions are not observed, *praying* can become an obstacle to attaining unconditional love. How this can happen will be taken up in a subsequent section.

Lord's Prayer

"You, therefore, should pray like this —

'Our Father, who is in heaven,
may your name be held holy,
   your kingdom come, your will be done —
on earth, as in heaven.
   Give us today
the bread that we will need;
   and forgive us our wrong-doings,
as we have forgiven those who have wronged us;
   and take us not into temptation,
but deliver us from evil.'" (Matthew 6:9-13 OEB)

"When you pray," Jesus answered, "say —
   'Father,
May your name be held holy,
your kingdom come.
   Give us each day the bread that we will need;
   and forgive us our sins,

for we ourselves forgive everyone who wrongs
us;
and take us not into temptation.'" (Luke 11:2-4
OEB)

Matthew 6:9-13 has a parallel in Luke 11:2-4, which is significantly shorter. Since it is unlikely that either evangelist would remove material if it were available, we conclude that Matthew added verses to this prayer rather than that Luke took any out. It is also likely that the source of this prayer for Matthew, as perhaps for Luke, was not a written document, but the prayer as it was said by Christians at the writer's time.

The word *Father* that Jesus used was the word *Abba*, which could be translated more appropriately as *Daddy*. The familiarity denoted by the word is far more important than the fact that the word is masculine.

"To hallow" a name or make it holy was best done by dying for that name. It would also seem that one would only do so if one could lay claim to that name, such as by being part of a family or nation. Consequently, the prayer implies bearing the name oneself as well as a willingness to die it.

In the Gospels the word for *kingdom* has an active meaning and is better translated by a word like *reign*.

"Thy will be done" is not part of Luke's prayer, but it is a logical extension of "Thy kingdom (reign) come."

The word for *daily* has had various translations, such as *supersubstantial*. Because of the way it was used elsewhere, it is perhaps best translated as "for tomorrow." Its use gives us the notion that God not only provides for today's needs, but is one step ahead by taking care of tomorrow's needs as well.

The "trial" seems to be the apocalyptic time Jesus referred to elsewhere. Consequently, it may be best translated as "Trial," capitalized. Since that Trial did not come to pass, we today can think of it as being our own personal time of trial. The petition containing this word certainly does not imply that God leads anyone into temptation or time of testing. Instead, it should be translated in such a way as asking God not to let us fall or fail.

The following is one way of translating the Lord's Prayer in such a way as to stay as close as possible to what are the original words of the prayer:

> Abba, Daddy,
> Your name is our sacred banner.
> Come, rule over us.
> Give us today our bread for tomorrow.
> Forgive us as we forgive others.
> And don't let us fail you when the Trial
>   comes.

In this poem an extra stanza is added as the doxology.

Beyond the reaches of the farthest galaxy,
enclosed in heart of earth beneath the sea,
you dwell in fulness not contained by bonds of space
or time. And yet within our tiny heart's embrace,
you also live, so close it seems but fantasy.
O Source of all, be at our side in all we do.
Please keep us always, in your kindness, close to you.

Your name is sacred, hallowed, holy, held by all
as glory-filled, beyond the honors that befall
the greatest of our human heroes here on earth.
And yet, as children, whom you fathered, have a birth
divine, we dare upon your name to proudly call.
O Father, since from you your name is ours to wear,
please grant that we your name will always proudly bear.

You rule the earth, the sky, the universe, the sea,
and land and all that dwell therein. You know and see
what's best for us; and to your wisdom far beyond
our grasp, we ask that we may faithfully respond.
Unless your will be done we never can be free.
O Wisdom, come and reign o'er each and every one.
We trust your plan for us. We pray your will be done.

We're anxious not for what we eat, for what to wear,
for what the day will bring. Indeed, our every hair
your mother's love has numbered. Daily bread we pray
from you, but trustful, we pray not for just this day,
but also for tomorrow. Mother, hear our prayer.
O Mother, caring, watching, sharing, us imbue
with your compassion. Make us kind like you.

Forgive our debts, we beg of you; our wrongs delete
from sight. We seek forgiveness for the way we treat
each other. Mercy flows like sunshine from your heart,
embracing ours. This light to us you will impart,
if we in turn forgive the debts of all we meet.
O Mercy without limit, blot out our sins from view.
Instill in us your kindness; make us just like you.

Our time of testing's sure to come; it may come soon
or late. We are your vines, so take your shears, and prune
us to bear fruit. Whate'er may be our purpose here,
renew our strength, let us not fail, destroy our fear,
and to your melody of peace our hearts attune.
O Light that beams through tunnel dark, light up our way
to guide us through the night, to fail you not this day.

By you begotten, sons and daughters, fruit of birth
divine, we've come each one of us to find our path on earth
to take us back to you. From heaven's home you see
us prodigals. You make our dreams reality
and turn our days of sorrow into joy and mirth.
O Source of all, all glory be forever yours. And may
our love for you not end. Please help us find the way.

Part VI

Loving:

Showing Love

by Doing

19

The First Commandment

When a scribe asked Jesus what was the first commandment, Jesus quoted Deuteronomy 6:4-5: to love God with
your whole heart, your whole soul, your whole mind, and
with all your heart. Then he quoted Leviticus 19:18 to say
that the second commandment was to love your neighbor as yourself.

> Then came up one of the teachers of the Law who
> had heard their discussions. Knowing that Jesus
> had answered them wisely, he asked him this
> question, "Which commandment is the most im-
> portant of all?
>
> "The most important," answered Jesus, "is —
> 'Hear, Israel; the Lord our God is the one Lord;
> and you must love the Lord your God with all your
> heart, and with all your soul, and with all your
> mind, and with all your strength.' The second is

this — 'You must love your neighbor as you love yourself.' There is no commandment greater than these."

"Wisely answered, teacher!" exclaimed the teacher of the Law. "It is true, as you say, that there is one God, and that there is no other besides him; and to love him with all one's heart, and with all one's understanding, and with all one's strength, and to love one's neighbor as one loves oneself is far beyond all burnt offerings and sacrifices."

Seeing that he had answered with discernment, Jesus said to him, "You are not far from the kingdom of God." (Mark 12:28-34, OEB)[45]

For Jesus, just keeping the Ten Commandments is not enough to gain eternal life.[46] Love fulfills all other commandments and sums up our purpose in life. The five practices previously enumerated, *perceiving, forgiving, blessing, giving thanks and praying* are stepping stones in practicing unconditional love.

Love, as our purpose in life, is not to be understood as a feeling or emotion, even though our emotions are good and helpful. It is, furthermore, as we understand from the verses in Mark, something different from, and superior to, offering worship and sacrifices. Love entails doing. Feeling love and saying we love are not enough to fulfill Jesus's two great commandments; we must put our feelings and words into action.

When faced with hatred and cruelty, is unconditional love possible? An example of a loving response in the worst circumstances is related by George G. Ritchie, who served in the army in World War II and became a prominent psychiatrist in Virginia. After the war was

---

[45] See also Matthew 22:34-40 and Luke 10:25-28.
[46] Mark 10:17-22.

over, Ritchie was assigned to work in a liberated concentration camp. To help the former inmates, whose lives had been shattered, the soldiers relied heavily on one of them, a man they called Wild Bill, who sported a handlebar mustache and whose Polish name they could not pronounce.

Wild Bill, the soldiers guessed, had not been in the camp very long. He stood erect, his eyes were bright, he was cheerful, and he was an excellent arbitrator in dealing with the former prisoners. Besides, he was fluent in English, French, German, and Russian, as well as his native Polish. Wild Bill worked up to sixteen hours a day, not showing fatigue.

One day Ritchie came across Wild Bill's papers; to his astonishment, he discovered that he had been imprisoned at the camp as one of the first prisoners in 1939. He stood out even from those imprisoned for just a short time.

Wild Bill told Ritchie his story. He and his family had lived in the Jewish section of Warsaw when the German soldiers took the captives and lined them up along the street. Because he spoke German, he was separated from his wife, his two daughters, and three small boys. Then he witnessed the German soldiers massacre everyone, including all in his family, with machine guns. His words voiced the impossible: "Hate had just killed the six people who mattered most to me in the world. I decided then that I would spend the rest of my life—whether it was a few days or many years—loving every person I came in contact with."[47]

---

[47] George G. Ritchie with Elizabeth Sherrill, *Return from Tomorrow,* Fleming H. Revell Company, Old Tappan, New Jersey, 1978, page 116.

20

Jesus as the Model for Love

There are multiple accounts of Jesus's service to the poor, the sick and the disabled. He healed and defended them. Here we will put these stories aside and concentrate on his death. Jesus was murdered, and the motive for his murder can reveal much about how he lived and what he hoped to accomplish. For example, from those who spouted hatred of Dr. Martin Luther King Jr., we can learn the motive for his assassination, which is that he was killed for championing the civil and human rights of both blacks and all oppressed people of his time.

Similarly, we can examine the motive for the murder of Jesus to see what it was in his life that spawned such malice. Rather than look at the legal reasons given to Pontius Pilate or the false accusations made against him while before the Sanhedrin, we will examine the motive in the minds of his murderers.

The basic elements of this story are explained in the account of the Cleansing of the Temple.

21

The Cleansing of the Temple

The Cleansing of the Temple was the event in Jesus's ministry that marked him for execution. It is recorded in all four Gospels, but the variations in each account necessitate deciding which evangelist's version is more historically accurate.[48]

John's version is unique by its placement of the story at the beginning of Jesus's ministry rather than at the end. The reason seems to be theological. The literary pattern of this Gospel stresses the theme that Jesus consistently worked miracles or "signs" to prove his mission. The Jews ask Jesus what sign he can show for his action.[49] This in turn enables John to turn the conversation into

---

[48] The four versions of the Cleansing of the Temple are found in Mark 11:15-19, Matthew 21:12-16, Luke 19:45-48, and John 2:13-22.
[49] John 2:18.

Jesus's prediction of his most significant sign, his resurrection.

The only addition John makes to the account is to say that Jesus made a whip of cords. We do not know the source of the evangelist's data, and most scholars surmise that he relates the same event as recorded in the other Gospels, only placed in a different time period. Since John was written at the end of the first century, a full generation after the other Gospels, it is the least preferred for historical testimony.

Mark is the earliest Gospel, from which Luke and Matthew copied. Each of these two shortened the story while adding no new details. Because Mark is the earliest source, it is preferable to the other Gospels for historical reliability.

For Mark, the Cleansing of the Temple is the turning point in the Gospel. Everything was going smoothly through Jesus's triumphal entry into Jerusalem; but right after the cleansing, the chief priests and scribes were looking for a way to kill him.

> They came to Jerusalem. Jesus went into the Temple Courts, and began to drive out those who were buying and selling there. He overturned the tables of the money changers, and the seats of the pigeon-dealers, and would not allow anyone to carry anything across the Temple Courts. Then he began to teach. "Does not scripture say," he asked, "'My house will be called a house of prayer for all the nations'? But you have made it a den of robbers." Now the chief priests and the teachers of the Law heard this and began to look for some way of putting Jesus to death; for they were afraid of him, since all the people were greatly impressed by his teaching. (Mark 11:15-18, OEB)

This event can be outlined as follows:

1. Jesus enters the temple and drives out those who were selling and buying.
2. He overturns the tables of the money changers and the chairs of those selling doves.
3. He does not allow anyone to carry anything through the temple precincts.
4. He quotes Isaiah 56:7: God's house shall be called a house of prayer; but he adds that those he is encountering have made it a den of thieves.
5. The chief priests and scribes hear of this, but we do not know how long afterward. Mark says that they continued to look for a way to kill him. This implies that they had already had this in mind, but now they had made a definitive decision. They were afraid of Jesus, but the reason for their fear is not stated.

The Temple Mount

To put Mark's account of the Cleansing of the Temple into its historical context, we need to describe its locale. The whole structure of its occurrence is called the Temple Mount, which stood thirty meters or ten stories above ground level. The top floor was an immense plaza in trapezoidal shape, measuring approximately 533 yards on the western wall, 503 on the eastern, 345 on the northern and 306 on the southern. The area was over 172,000 square yards, big enough to hold twenty American football fields and one hundred thousand people.

Off center, running from east to west, with more open space on the south, was the temple complex or building, which only Jews could enter. The Holy of Holies was at the west end of the building, and at the east was the entrance, leading first to the Court of the Women, then to other areas for men, Levites and priests. The entire open area outside the Temple building was the Court of the Gentiles.

Most scholars place the Cleansing of the Temple in the mammoth Court of the Gentiles. The rooms inside the temple building were too small to house any significant number of businesses or tables for money changers.

Mark says that Jesus "would not allow anyone to carry anything across the Temple Courts." How Jesus could accomplish this is puzzling. The Court of the Gentiles is so vast that no one person could have covered the entire area or guarded both sides of the temple structure at the same time. Nor could Jesus have blocked all the gates into the area. To keep people from entering the Court of the Gentiles, he would have had to block four gates on the north and two on the south. His followers could possibly have aided him.

On the other hand, the other actions of Jesus make sense. He drove out those who were buying and selling, and overturned the tables of the money changers. All this took place in the Court of the Gentiles and not in the temple building.

Since the Cleansing of the Temple took place in the Court of the Gentiles, Jesus must have been demanding that the entire Temple Mount should be kept holy and not just the temple itself. Jesus was teaching that the temple should be a house of prayer for all the nations. However, it is unlikely that Jesus would have demanded that all businesses be banned from the plaza or Court of the Gentiles area. The Temple Mount was built with the plaza area, especially around the perimeter, to be a place for markets and businesses. It would have been similar in use to a Roman forum.

Overseeing the Temple Mount was a tower with Roman sentries who could oversee all that was happening there. We have no record that they intervened, even though any serious disturbance in or outside the temple could result in Roman armed intervention. We have no hint in the Gospels that Jesus was rebelling against Rome or had any intention to do so. Since the chief priests and scribes apparently heard of Jesus's protest after it was over, we have to search for another motive for murdering him besides fear of Roman intervention.

Jesus's Protest

There would have been many commercial groups or markets in the huge expanse surrounding the temple, but the ones Jesus protested were those selling animals for sacrifice. Pilgrims came from afar to offer their sacrifices, which required animals without blemish of any kind. Travel made it difficult to transport any animals, and especially hard to keep animals in perfect condition. Those selling animals, then, offered a valuable service. What was unconscionable was that the sacrificial animals were often sold at prices exorbitantly inflated.

The other group that angered Jesus was that of the money changers. Like those selling animals, they too were carrying out an essential function for the temple. It was their job to collect the temple tax, which was to be paid once a year by every adult male. They began their work each year in various locations throughout the country and set up tables in the Temple Mount only a short time before Passover. They collected the tax from those who had not yet paid and changed foreign and local money into the coinage required for any offering going to the temple. This enabled pilgrims from outside territories to exchange their coins for the acceptable temple coinage.

The requirement for a specific kind of coin for temple commerce necessitated money changers. The only coin acceptable was minted in Tyre and called the Tyrian tetradrachma, or sometimes the Tyrian shekel or silver shekel. The Tyrian coin was chosen because of its purity, being close to 95 percent pure silver. It was stamped with the figure of a pagan god (Heracles/Hercules), which should have made it unacceptable; but the temple authorities judged the coin's purity to be more important.

The tax for adult males was a half shekel. To make sure that at least a half shekel was being paid, the tax collectors (or money changers) charged a small extra payment, part of which was to pay the money changers for their work.

Tetradrachma literally means four drachmas. Since one drachma seems to have been a day's wages for a Roman soldier or for a worker in a vineyard, half a Tyrian tetradrachma has been equated with wages for two days.

This equivalency is not the whole picture. A Roman soldier may have received a drachma as a daily wage, but Jewish peasants had no guarantee of being employed every day. This is especially true of farmers and peasants, such as those in Galilee and other territories outside Judea, who found it difficult to come up with a half Tyrian tetradrachma. Besides, the coin was not used in daily commerce by the Jews, who had to go to a money changer to purchase one either for the temple tax or for an animal sacrifice. The need for a Tyrian tetradrchma was an added hardship for the many Jews living on the edge.

The ancient law requiring a tax to be paid to the temple specified that it be paid only once in a lifetime, when an adult male reached the age of twenty. By the first century, sometime after the Maccabean revolt, the law had been expanded to demand payment annually after the age of twenty. The burden on the poor must have been one of the reasons for Jesus's anger.

Jesus himself was one of the poor. He[50] and his father Joseph[51] are each described in Greek as a *tektōn,* universally translated as carpenter, but whose actual meaning is more likely to be a laborer or someone who works with his hands. The traditional translation as carpenter is misplaced, because there would have been little wood to work with in Nazareth. But *tektōn* certainly does not mean an artisan or skilled workman. Jesus came from Nazareth in Galilee, and he preached mainly to Galileans. There was no middle class there. A few were wealthy, but most were poor, living on the edge, a little above the subsistence level. Jesus was one of these, and he identified with them.

Follow the Money

Jesus did not directly attack the chief priests and scribes, but rather merchants and money changers. The priests did not resolve to correct the abuses Jesus challenged, but reacted by treating his protest as directed personally at them. They asked Jesus to tell them by what authority he acted.[52] By defending their authority, they admitted that they were responsible for the businesses and money changers operating in the temple. The primary ones to blame, then, were the chief priests and elders in charge of the temple.

Someone was making huge profits from the temple businesses that Jesus protested, so we need to follow

---

[50] Mark 6:3.
[51] Matthew 13:33.
[52] Mark 11:21.

the money. The temple had expenses to meet, but in contrast to the poor and the common people in Israel, there was an aristocratic class that had wealth beyond the dreams of anyone else. These were the temple priests.

When Jerusalem was destroyed in 70 CE, it was unlivable; and most had either deserted or been killed. But through archeological research in the city, we have learned much about the lives of the temple priests. Their homes were prime real estate, located on a hill west of the temple, with a sublime vista of the temple and the city, and enjoying a cooling breeze during most of the year.

The homes in (what is now called) the Jewish Quarter were destroyed by the Romans in 70 CE, but excavations reveal much about the inhabitants' lifestyle. The houses had marble panels and frescoes, beautiful mosaic floors, and were decorated in the latest Roman styles, except that there were no figured images because of religious prohibitions. The homes were also distinguished by numerous Jewish ritual baths.

The elite enjoyed an expensive Second Pompeian type of decorations and living quarters, including the best imported dinner ware and stone furniture. One singular find was a broken vase by Ennion, a renowned glass blower in Phoenicia, north of Israel. Among the archeological finds are examples of the best imported glassware and dishes.

In one of the homes excavated in the Jewish quarter the words *Bar Kathros* were found inscribed in stone. Since Kathros was the name of a priestly family, we know for certain that the priests lived among the very wealthy. The temple priests, together with the Sadducees, comprised a social class with a life of luxury on a par with the richest in the Roman Empire. All of this was supported under the auspices of religion.

In recent times archeologists discovered an ossuary, or stone box for the bones of the deceased, with the
name of Caiaphas inscribed on it. This has been universally accepted as the burial box of Caiaphas, the high
priest at the time of Jesus, and of his family. Only the very
rich had ossuaries, and this ossuary shows that Caiaphas
was one of them.

Why was Jesus murdered? Mark gives us the key
in understanding why Jesus's ministry turned from a cel-
ebratory welcome into Jerusalem into a decision to put
him to death. He exposed the evils going on in the name
of religion. He challenged those responsible. He pitted
himself directly against the wealthy and powerful, and he
took the side of the poor and oppressed. He defended the
temple as a loyal and faithful Jew, but protested the use
of political and religious power to oppress his people.
Those in authority saw the murder of Jesus as the only
way to eliminate the threat to curtail their cash flow and
their luxurious life style.

Jesus was crucified because he defended the poor,
the outcasts, and the oppressed. We can find no better
expression of love in action than how he suffered and
died on behalf of others.

To follow Jesus demands love — especially of the
poor; and love demands action.

22

The Spiritual Practice of

Loving by Acting

Infusing our actions with love requires correct thinking. If we have fallen into thinking that some persons do not deserve our love, we need to remind ourselves that everyone is a child of God and therefore lovable. If we have injuries that make us think only of punishment and returning injury for injury, it is time to recall that we must forgive to be forgiven. And if we believe our oppressor deserves to be injured, we must offer a blessing instead. In other words, to practice love habitually, it is necessary to think correctly by practicing *perceiving, forgiving, blessing, giving thanks,* and *praying.*

To love is our purpose in life, and as such requires habitual practice. It may be that there is someone in your life whom you find it especially hard to love. Just as it is easier to acquire the habit of forgiving by starting with small offenses, it is easier to make love habitual by working first in small steps. Make a practice of doing one small favor for someone at least once each day. Try to do so, at least some of the time, without letting anyone be aware and without being thanked. If helpful, mark your calendar each day if you have succeeded.

If you have wronged others in any way, keep in mind the law of cause and effect — that you reap what you sow. Even if you have been forgiven, harm to others incurs a debt to be repaid. Unconditional love demands atonement insofar as possible.

Be honest with yourself, acknowledging when you have failed to help someone in need. Although it is essential to take care of yourself and your family first, look also to those in your neighborhood and beyond. We are all interconnected, both spiritually and socially, so that what helps or harms one person ripples across all societies and peoples.

Jesus identified with outcasts and oppressed, and he was murdered because he defied the temple priests who were using religious legalisms to steal from the poor. Select a social cause of your choice, and contribute whatever you can to further that cause, whether it be monetary or a donation of your time and effort. To love Jesus, love the poor.

Some persons are caregivers whose time is consumed by providing for a disabled or sick loved one. Some struggle to provide food and clothing for their family. Others may find themselves with time and money to spare. You alone can decide the ways you can show generosity. If you are among the needy, perhaps you can join with others in like circumstances to improve each other's lives.

Meditate on these ideas: Life is a gift in which we have the opportunity to grow in love. Just as we reap what we sow when we do wrong, we also reap our reward by loving.

"Do not store up treasures for yourselves on earth, where moth and rust destroy, and where thieves break in and steal. But store up treasures for yourselves in heaven, where neither moth nor rust destroys, and where thieves do not break in or steal. For where your treasure is, there will your heart be also." (Matthew 6:19-21, OEB)

"Blessed are the poor in spirit,
for theirs is the kingdom of heaven.
Blessed are the mourners,
for they will be comforted.
Blessed are the gentle,
for they will inherit the earth.
Blessed are those who hunger and thirst for righteousness,
for they will be satisfied.
Blessed are the merciful,
for they will find mercy.
Blessed are the pure in heart,
for they will see God.
Blessed are the peacemakers,
for they will be called children of God.
Blessed are those who have been persecuted in the cause of righteousness,
for theirs is the kingdom of heaven.

"Blessed are you when people insult you, and persecute you, and say all kinds of evil lies about you because of me. Be glad and rejoice, because your reward in heaven will be great; this is the way they persecuted the prophets who lived before you." (Matthew 5:3-12, OEB)

Your Notebook

The bigger your goals, the more helpful it is to write them down. Your successes can be a starting point: What are you good at doing? How have you helped others in the past? Review the needs of those near to you and of your community. How can you use your abilities to remedy any of their needs?

Prioritize what you can do and want to do: Where can you be the most effective? What are the greatest needs?

Choose one or two goals to work on to avoid spreading yourself too thin. This is true as well for your monetary contributions. No one can donate to all who make requests, no matter how worthy the cause. Decide which causes are most significant to you.

Your primary goals will be carried over from day to day; other minor goals, like visiting a sick friend or helping a child with homework, you may enter in your notebook as a to-do list.

Use your notebook in any way that helps you. Do not be discouraged if you fail to accomplish all the goals you write down. Use your list of goals to see what is realistic for you.

Invitation

Then Jesus went on to say to the man who had invited him, "When you give a breakfast or a dinner, do not ask your friends, or your brothers or sisters, or your relatives, or rich neighbors, because they might invite you in return, and so you should be repaid. No, when you entertain, invite the poor, the crippled, the lame, the blind; and then you will be happy indeed, since they cannot reward you; for you will be rewarded at the resurrection of the good." (Luke 14:12-14 OEB)

The following poem is a tribute to my mother, who by word and example taught me compassion and love in action. In the first and second stanzas I recall the depression days of the late 1930s as I grew up in Kansas. The third stanza depicts memories of the early forties at the end of World War II.

At the back door they'd come knocking, wearing rags and
    seeking food.
"We'll mow your lawn or weed your garden, trim your
    bushes, chop some wood."

In the midst of the depression, wandering far without
    suitcase,
hobos begged for food and coffee, riding rails from place to
    place.

They'd find our home but skip our neighbors', knowing we
    would treat them well.
It's said they somehow marked the homes where kind and
    loving folk would dwell.

For kind and loving was my mother to those tired and
    hungry men.
She always could find food for them, no matter how, no
    matter when.

She'd make a sandwich, pour some coffee, maybe serve
    them apple pie;
an extra sandwich for their trip — their daily bread she
    would supply.

If she were living, she would tell me, "You don't need to
    give the best;
you just give the best you have, and then you're sure to
    pass the test.

"Reward from God does not depend on candles lit or linens
    pressed.
Instead, be sure you feed the homeless and the lonely and
    depressed.

"It's not the fancy foods you serve that show how much you
care;
it's the people you invite and the neediness of those with
whom you share."

A little later, times were better: beggars few and far
between.
Still, poverty was living there, though hardly heard and
barely seen.

My older brother told my mother, "I've a friend whose
family
has little food, no Christmas gifts, no money for a
Christmas tree."

My mother quickly searched our house — each cupboard,
every drawer;
and then some gifts, like toys and dolls, came from my
father's ten-cent store.

My mother to the grocery store my older brother sent,
then once the gifts were wrapped and packed, on
pilgrimage we went.

'Twas getting dark on Christmas Eve. We drove until we
found
their house — a basement house — one built beneath the
ground.

My brother and my mother were the messengers of grace.
I only watched them from the car—a memory I can't erase.

If she were living, she would say, "You need not give the
best.
You just give the best you have, and then you'll pass the
test.

*"Some people live in mansions, filled with leather chairs
    and chrome.
But basement huts with floors of dirt, love can make into a
    home.*

*"God's reward does not depend on chandeliers or
    silverware.
No, serve the outcasts and neglected — their rejections
    with them share.*

*"It's not your linen tablecloths that show how much you
    care;
it's the people you invite and the neediness of those with
    whom you share."*

In South Dakota in the forties, every Sunday we would
    take
a picnic to the mountains, Custer Park, or Sylvan Lake.

Not afraid to pick up strangers, we'd offer anyone a ride.
Most of all we'd pick up soldiers, share our chicken,
    Southern fried.

I was the only one at home — my brothers all had gone to
    war.
To substitute, three servicemen would meet us at my
    father's store.

My mother early every Sunday fixed a picnic lunch
    sublime;
chicken, rolls, and ice cream made a perfect summertime.

When summertime was over, in that August, war was won.
We had to picnic by ourselves, for the servicemen had
    gone.

156

If my mother were alive, I'm sure that she'd have this to
    say,
"Share with others while you can, and enjoy the present
    day.

"It doesn't matter what you share, you need not give the
    best.
You just give the best you have, and then you'll pass the
    test.

"Don't worry when the ones you help have no way to
    repay.
Be happy when the ones you touch enjoy a joyful day.

"If you seek repayment here, you give it up hereafter.
Instead, serve those who can't repay, in cheerfulness and
    laughter.

"It's not the cost of food and time that shows how much
    you care;
it's the people you invite and the neediness of those with
    whom you share.

Part VII

Obstacles and Illusions

23

The Eye of a Needle

As Jesus was resuming his journey, a man came running up to him, and threw himself on his knees before him. "Good teacher," he asked, "what must I do to gain eternal life?"

> "Why do you call me good?" answered Jesus. "No one is good but God. You know the commandments — 'Do not kill. Do not commit adultery. Do not steal. Do not say what is false about others. Do not cheat. Honor your father and your mother.'"

> "Teacher," he replied, "I have observed all these from my childhood."

> Jesus looked at the man, and his heart went out to him, and he said, "There is still one thing wanting in you; go and sell all that you have, and give to the poor, and you will have wealth in heaven; then come and follow me." But the man's face clouded at these words, and he went away distressed, for he had great possessions. (Mark 10:17-22, OEB)

The encounter with the rich man gave Jesus an opportunity to teach his disciples about the dangers of wealth:

> Then Jesus looked around, and said to his disciples, "How hard it will be for people of wealth to enter the kingdom of God!" The disciples were amazed at his words. But Jesus said again, "My children, how hard a thing it is to enter the kingdom of God! It is easier for a camel to get through a needle's eye, than for a rich person to enter the kingdom of God."
>
> "Then who can be saved?" they exclaimed in the greatest astonishment.
>
> Jesus looked at them, and answered, "With people it is impossible, but not with God; for everything is possible with God." (Mark 10:23-27, OEB)[53]

Various explanations have been given for this comparison. One of the most popular is that there was a gate (in or near Jerusalem?) named "Eye of a Needle," which was so narrow that camels had to unload their wares to pass through, making a caravan an easy target for bandits. There is, however, little or no evidence for such a gate.

---

[53] See also Matthew 19:23-26; Luke 18:24-26.

Some Greek linguists point out that the Greek word for camel, *kamelos,* differs by only one letter from the word for rope, *kamilos.* Consequently, it is possible that biblical copyists got the wrong word. This is unlikely, since the word for rope appears in none of the ancient manuscripts.

A third possibility is that the Greek does not accurately reflect the saying of Jesus, who spoke Aramaic. According to George M. Lamsa, "The Aramaic word *gamla* means *rope* and *camel.*"[54] Lamsa translates Matthew 20:24 with the word *rope* instead of *camel.* (The Aramaic word may have had two definitions because camel hair could have been used to make rope.)

Perhaps the most likely explanation for Jesus's words is that he was using a common proverb. The Babylonian Talmud[55] has a parallel saying about an elephant being brought through the eye of a needle. In Judea elephants were never seen, whereas camels, as the largest animal to pass through the country, would have been more fitting to express something impossible.

Whatever our explanation of the biblical text, Jesus is expressing how extremely difficult wealth makes it for anyone to enter the kingdom of heaven; but he also adds that with God all things are possible.

Money, though, is not the only obstacle on our path to achieve unconditional love. In the following chapters we will look at some of the ways we can be led astray and away from our ultimate goal.

---

[54] *Holy Bible From the Ancient Eastern Text, George M. Lamsa's Translations From the Aramaic of the Peshitta,* Harper-SanFrancisco, 1968, page 974. The quotation is a footnote to Matthew 20:24.

[55] *Berakoth,* 55b.

24

Time

The Synoptic Gospels (Matthew, Mark and Luke) begin with a call to *metanoia,* translated as *repentance,* but literally meaning a change of mind or a change in one's way of thinking. A cursory reading of the Gospels, such as the Sermon on the Mount in Matthew, underscores the need for a radical change in our values. Underpinning our values, however, is the change made by Jesus in how we view time.

As stated earlier, all of Jesus's teachings were made with the conviction that the kingdom of God was to appear immediately, even within the lifetimes of some of his hearers.[56] Notwithstanding the fact that this predic-

---

[56] Mark 9:1.

tion was not fulfilled, the implications of Jesus's proclamations on the transitoriness of this world require a specific way of thinking.

How we view time is critical to our spiritual progress. Even though everyone acknowledges that life eventually comes to an end, there is the constant illusion that there is always more of it to come, so that we still have more time to enjoy our possessions and to accomplish our goals.

Jesus was not silent on this tendency:

> Then Jesus told them this parable — "There was once a rich man whose land was very fertile; and he began to ask himself 'What will I do, for I have nowhere to store my crops? This is what I will do,' he said; 'I will pull down my barns and build larger ones, and store all my grain and my goods in them; and I will say to myself, Now you have plenty of good things put by for many years; take your ease, eat, drink, and enjoy yourself.' But God said to the man 'Fool! This very night your life is being demanded; and as for all you have prepared — who will have it?' So it is with those who lay by wealth for themselves and are not rich to the glory of God." (Luke 12:16-21, OEB)

The illusion of time goes beyond thinking that there is always time to spare; it leads us to think that time is ours and ours alone. We fail to understand that time, like material possessions, must be shared with others.

25

Separation

The most misleading illusion, and one of the hardest to overcome, is separation. Our physical vision interprets reality is a conglomerate of individual parts, with humanity as a multitude of individual, totally independent persons. The illusion of complete separation from others, if not counteracted by the deliberate practice of *perceiving*, can become a nightmare.

We are by nature social beings. At times we all need private time, but to live without social contact is nearly impossible. Astronauts endure solitary flights for only a limited time, and are never sent into space for prolonged periods without companions. Christian hermits may be one of the exceptions to the norm of social living, but we cannot be sure to what extent these men and women were really able to avoid social contact. Some gained a following from those seeking spiritual guidance.

Some sold items in cities so they could buy food. And some gathered from time to time to celebrate a common liturgy. Those who lived without making any human contact were rare exceptions.

For the other ninety-nine percent of humanity social contact is an absolute necessity; even the Christian hermits of the Egyptian desert were raised in families and in a social setting before seeking a life of extreme asceticism. It is in our nature to want to belong — to a family, a society, a group of friends, a nation, a religion, or an organization with common beliefs or interests. Other people give meaning to our lives. To cut someone off from all human contact, as in solitary confinement, is one of the cruelest human punishments ever devised.

The illusion of separation from others is a constant and vicious attack on life itself, and especially on our spiritual path. Separation is used as punishment from the earliest ages: "Go to your room." It is judged as normal to temporarily cut a child off from being a part of the family as punishment for misbehavior. The practice of excluding others from one's group reinforces the illusion of being separated and without need of others. Such exclusion reaches an extreme form in the penalty of excommunication by some religious groups — groups which ought to be models of inclusion.

Taunting, ridicule, and alienation are practices used to put down those who are different in any way: nationality, race, gender, sexual orientation, religious beliefs, or multiple kinds of handicaps. To tell someone — in any way — that one is not an acceptable member of society, is a devastating form of cruelty that often leads to suicide, especially among the young.

For many reasons the illusion of separation is one of the most difficult obstacles to overcome in order to reach our ultimate goal of unconditional love.

26

Death

The popular beliefs about death are many. We do not know what our ancestors thousands of years ago thought about death. They conducted burials and memorials, but it is uncertain what beliefs were symbolized. Ancestors were revered, but whether there was a belief that they lived on in any way other than through their descendants is unknown. For some death is the end, with no survival of consciousness.

Among Christians there are a variety of beliefs. The Catholic Church teaches that the human soul survives after death, but that the soul is not a complete human being until it is resurrected with its body on the final Day of Judgment. Some Christian churches teach that after death we are unconscious — as if asleep — until judgment day.

Scientists offer mixed opinions. While some say that it is impossible to know whether the soul or consciousness survives after death, others differ, even stating that consciousness (though not defined) must survive. Some notable scientists, such as Max Planck, assert that consciousness is the fundamental factor in the universe, so that matter derives from consciousness and not vice versa.

Christians have always accepted some kind of life after death because of their belief in the resurrection of Jesus. The idea of the resurrection of the dead was first firmly declared in the book of Daniel, although there were already hints of this in Ezekiel. In the Old Testament we have the story of Saul consulting a medium to talk to the deceased prophet Samuel.[57]

There is a long tradition of people trying to communicate with the dead. Joan of Arc had visions of Archangel Michael, Saint Margaret, and Saint Catherine of Alexandria, who advised her on her military mission. Throughout the 1800s mediums were popular; Abraham Lincoln consulted Spiritualistic mediums — a fact ignored in American history textbooks.

In the past decades, an explosion in after-death studies has taken place. Near-death experiences, a term popularized by Dr. Raymond Moody, are now so ingrained in American consciousness that nearly everyone recognizes what is meant by going through a tunnel and seeing the light. The number of near-death experiencers in the United States is estimated at over four million, and bookstores sell hundreds of books that give detailed accounts of NDEs and documented sociological, psychological and medical studies of what people went through in

---

[57] 1 Samuel 28.

an NDE and how they changed afterward, often under-taking a new spiritual path or developing psychic abili-ties.

Mediums vary in their reliability. The most repu-table can claim to give information from the deceased that they have no way of knowing through natural means. Some of them have undergone double-blind stud-ies to verify their work.

There is also a multitude of books available on af-ter-death communications, past-life regression therapy, and encounters — sometimes life-saving — with angels.

Many scientists, along with others, dismiss all of these studies and literature on the grounds that results cannot be replicated and thus be subject to proof by the scientific method. In reply, anecdotal evidence, which in-cludes the testimony of witnesses, is overwhelming, and overwhelmingly consistent.

Under the "Suggested Reading" section at the end of this book are numerous books pertaining to life after death. Many are anecdotal, but some are controlled, sci-entific studies, which are worth examining and taking se-riously. Without a knowledgeable view of death, we are apt to yield to the illusion that death is an ending, thereby missing the perception of death as a transition, and we will fail to perceive that we remain spiritually united with our departed loved ones even though they are no longer physically present.

27

False Values

Wealth

Jesus was clear on the danger wealth poses to spiritual values:

> "No one can serve two masters, for either they will hate one and love the other, or else they will attach themselves to one and despise the other. You cannot serve both God and Money." (Matthew 6:24, OEB)

Jesus made his principle concrete, explaining that if our goal — or our heart — is centered on acquiring wealth, we fail to love God.

Material possessions cloud our judgment. They make it easy to follow the illusion that we can always acquire more, that more will make us happy, and that we have ample time to enjoy what we acquire.

> "Do not store up treasures for yourselves on earth, where moth and rust destroy, and where thieves break in and steal. But store up treasures for yourselves in heaven, where neither moth nor rust destroys, and where thieves do not break in or steal. For where your treasure is, there will your heart be also." (Matthew 6:19-21, OEB)

By placing a false value on material possessions, we slide into putting a false value on those who own them. The Epistle of James excoriates the abuses that must have been taking place at the time:

> My friends, are you really trying to combine faith in Jesus Christ, our glorified Lord, with discrimination? Suppose a visitor should enter your synagogue, with gold rings and in grand clothes, and suppose a poor man should come in also, in shabby clothes, and you show more respect to the visitor who is wearing grand clothes, and say — "There is a good seat for you here," but to the poor man — "You must stand; or sit down there by my footstool," Haven't you made distinctions among yourselves, and used evil standards of judgement? Listen, my dear friends. Has not God chosen those who are poor in the things of this world to be rich through their faith, and to possess the kingdom which he has promised to those who love him? But you — you insult the poor man! Isn't it the rich who oppress you? Isn't it they who drag you into law courts? Isn't it they who malign that honorable name spoken over you at your baptism? If you keep the royal law which runs — 'You must love your neighbor as you love yourself,' you are doing right; but, if you discriminate, you commit a sin, and stand convicted by that same

law of being offenders against it. (James 2:1-9,
OEB)

By placing a false value on our possessions, we fall
victim to putting an illusory value on people, so that we
falsely judge the rich to be greater and more important
than the poor. This is a failure in the practice of *perceiving*, whereby we acknowledge all others as equals, as our
sisters and brothers, and as God's children.

Jesus warned us not to judge others:

> "Do not judge and you will not be judged. For, just
> as you judge others, you will yourselves be
> judged, and the standard that you use will be
> used for you. Why do you look at the speck of
> sawdust in your friend's eye, while you pay no at-
> tention at all to the plank of wood in yours? How
> will you say to your friend 'Let me take out the
> speck from your eye,' when all the time there is a
> plank in your own? Hypocrite! Take out the plank
> from your own eye first, and then you will see
> clearly how to take out the speck from your
> friend's." (Matthew 7:1-5, OEB)

By judging others — ranking some as better or
worse than others — we close our minds to who we really are.

Paul likewise condemned the actions of the Corinthians who ate their full in celebrating the Last Supper
celebration, while leaving nothing for the poor.[58]

Physical Force

American culture is saturated with images of physical
prowess. Movies, comic books and video games offer su-
perheroes able to fly, repel bullets, walk through fire, and

---

[58] 1 Corinthians 11:17-22.

lay waste to hordes of soldiers, tanks and bombers. In the sports world we make heroes of those who excel in overpowering others in football, wrestling, boxing, and other arenas. Politicians in the United States remind their constituents that this country's military is the most powerful in the world.

The widespread and deeply ingrained ideal of physical power implants in our minds two grievously flawed illusions. The first is that we are not truly equal with others unless we are just as strong. There is the constant fear of being inferior, not just because we lose the race, do not make the team, or we cannot compete. On a wider and larger scale, we see the proliferation of weapons, such as handguns, so we can shoot first; or military armaments and nuclear weapons, so we can deter any nation or terrorist group that dares to anger us.

This illusion stands out in women's struggle for equality with men. While it is true that sexual equality demands that women be given equal opportunity to develop a career as a construction worker, as a soldier, as a firefighter, as a police officer, or in any other life path previously open only to men, it is also true that women (and men as well) who are unable or choose not to compete in such careers are nonetheless equal to those who do. Women must be treated as equal to men, because they *are* equal.

The second illusion is even more deadly. Our national obsession with physical power implicitly lures us to the false belief that by shooting the thief, incarcerating the murderer, or bombing terrorist headquarters, we are at the same time destroying evil itself. This kind of thinking can backfire, as Jesus warned,

> "Sheathe your sword," Jesus said, "for all who draw the sword will be put to the sword." (Matthew 26:52, OEB)

We dare not be deceived with the illusion that evil can be ultimately overcome by forceful retaliation. Jesus's message to love all others unconditionally, including our enemies, is the only true path, since God does not seek to destroy sinners, but to save them:

> So Jesus told them this parable — "Who among you who has a hundred sheep, and has lost one of them, does not leave the ninety-nine out in the open country, and go after the lost sheep until he finds it? And, when he has found it, he puts in on his shoulders rejoicing; and, on reaching home, he calls his friends and his neighbors together, and says 'Come and rejoice with me, for I have found my sheep which was lost.' So, I tell you, there will be more rejoicing in heaven over one outcast who repents, than over ninety-nine religious people, who have no need to repent. Or again, what woman who has ten silver coins, if she loses one of them, does not light a lamp, and sweep the house, and search carefully until she finds it? And, when she has found it, she calls her friends and neighbors together, and says 'Come and rejoice with me, for I have found the coin which I lost.' So, I tell you, there is rejoicing in the presence of God's angels over one outcast who repents." (Luke 15:3-10, OEB)

The adherents of the apocalyptic movement dreamt of the time when God would set the world straight by wreaking destruction on the Gentiles. In the book of Revelation, John of Patmos described numerous visions of such plagues and disasters. In chapter 9, we discover their purpose. The rest of humanity that were still alive had not repented, but, continuing in their sinful acts, had failed to repent. The purpose of the disasters was not punishment, but repentance.

> But those who were left of humanity, who had not
> perished through these curses, did not repent and
> turn away from what their own hands had made;
> they would not abandon the worship of demons,
> and of idols made of gold or silver or brass or
> stone or wood, which can neither see, nor hear,
> nor walk; and they did not repent of their murders,
> or their sorceries, or their licentiousness, or their
> thefts. (Revelation 9:20-21, OEB)

In the book of Revelation John of Patmos refuted the illusion that evil is overcome by force. He ended his book with a vision of evil being conquered by the sword from the mouth of the Lamb. In the numerous visions preceding the dramatic conclusion, plagues and disasters were poured out on the sinful Gentiles; none of them succeeded. From Revelation it is clear that the only way to conquer evil — whether in our own lives or in the world — is by implementing Jesus's message in our own lives. And Jesus's moral standard and ideal is the same for nations as for individuals.

Pleasure and Fame

All the pitfalls of the illusions of wealth are shared by other attractions, such as pleasure and fame. It is all too easy to think, and thus to act, as though our control over others, our fun time, or praise from others will last forever. All these, like our possessions, will be left behind when we breathe our last breath. And during this lifetime they will keep us from seeing the true value in others as God sees.

Attachment to fame, power, and riches leads to a false judgment of those who are poor, underprivileged, or unknown. In describing the final judgment, Jesus identifies with these outcasts: Whenever you feed the hungry, heal the sick, visit those in prison, or help the needy, you are doing it for Jesus himself.[59] For those who seek a personal relationship with Jesus, it is readily available in one's relationships with the poor and deprived.

If you are one of the needy or outcasts of society, know that God does not love you less and that God intends no one to be a victim. Join with others in similar situations and of like mind to help one another.

When we die, the only thing we can take with us is our relationships. We must make them good ones.

Prayer

Although *praying* is a spiritual practice leading us to the goal of unconditional love, it can also be an obstacle to that same goal, as Jesus warned:

> "And, when you pray, you are not to behave as hypocrites do. They like to pray standing in the synagogues and at the corners of the streets, so that people will see them. There, I tell you, is their reward! But, when one of you prays, they should go into their own room, shut the door, and pray to their Father who dwells in secret; and their Father, who sees what is secret, will reward them. When praying, do not repeat the same words over and over again, as is done by the Gentiles, who think that by using many words they will obtain a hearing. Do not imitate them; for God, your Father, knows what you need before you ask him." (Matthew 6:5-8, OEB)

Whether our times and formulas for prayer are dictated by ourselves or by some religious authority, our compliance is no indication of spiritual development. The recitation of daily prayers or the regular attendance at weekly religious services may be helpful, but they can

---

[59] Matthew 25:31-45.

also hide a misguided life. We must constantly test our sincerity.

The possible illusion of misguided prayer can also be found in the mastery of those abilities classified as psychic, such as healing, precognition, mediumship, and the like. Some persons regularly practice meditation and claim to have "raised their consciousness." There is no doubt that many of these persons have achieved experiences outside those of the average public. Without passing judgment on anyone who has had extraordinary spiritual experiences, these experiences should not be mistaken for the attainment of unconditional love. All spiritual experiences and psychic abilities can be aids in living a full spiritual life, and many who claim them use them unselfishly to benefit others; but we must not be misled by the illusion that having them is in itself a sign of spiritual fulfillment.

Besides the danger of using the façade of prayer as an illusion of spiritual progress, it is worthwhile here to recall the earlier warning (chapter 11) of Dr. Larry Dossey, who stated "that prayer can be used at a distance to *harm* people without their knowledge."[60]

---

[60] Larry Dossey, M.D., *Healing Words: The Power of Prayer and the Practice of Medicine,* HarperSanFrancisco, 1993, page 79.

28

Lack of Empathy

One of the most important building blocks in a child's de-velopment is the ability to distinguish one's right hand from the left. This achievement is a necessary in order to recognize that when you face another person, her right hand is on your left and her left hand is on your right. It is a learning process vital in being able to see the world from another's social, cultural, and mental perspective.

Unless we can see the world through the eyes of others, we cannot see how others perceive us, nor can we understand others' opinions or feelings. Lack of empathy allows us to believe the illusion that our feelings, our ideas, and our opinions are the only correct ones.

The consequence of a lack of empathy is to mis-judge ourselves and others. Jesus warns against this dan-ger in his admonition to get rid of the large plank in your own eye before criticizing the speck in the eye of an-other.[61]

All of us have experienced being put down by an-other. Even if we knew we had been at fault, we alone could know our concrete circumstances, our training and how we may have made a wrong decision, perhaps be-lieving we were doing something good. If we feel that no one can adequately judge us, then we must never act un-der the illusion that we can adequately judge anyone else.

The following are various ways in which we can fail to see reality from a differing point of view.

Revenge

Revenge, as already noted, necessitates the practice of forgiveness. It is also an obstacle to our spiritual growth by presenting the illusion that not only can we judge oth-ers, but we can punish them as well. Those seeking vengeance are acting out of an inability to perceive oth-ers as God sees them.

Fear

If you encounter a bear in the woods, your first inclina-tion is most likely to turn and run. Some advise the oppo-site: face the bear, make yourself look as big as possible, and make a lot of noise. While you are afraid of the bear, the bear may also fear you.

We have reason to fear a gunman in the middle of the night; fear of those of a different culture, race, reli-gion or sexual orientation is altogether different. Fear of the unknown, or of those you do not understand, derives

---

[61] Matthew 7:1-5.

from an illusion that you are safe only in your own familiar environment and with your own opinions.

Tommy Rosa, while undergoing a near-death experience, was given these words from his Teacher in 1999, "What you fear, you will draw to yourself. Remember this, because it is sacred knowledge."[62] This axiom is voiced by numerous spiritual and psychological authors. Fear becomes an obstacle to love by creating inaction. If we are afraid of failure, we fail to attempt being successful. Some physicians claim that negative emotions — and fear is one of them — can induce illness. Worst of all, fear can keep you from having full confidence and faith in your Father.

To act out of fear of others is to prejudge them without sufficient knowledge. It may even be a fear of recognizing being wrong. Some psychologists and spiritual writers propose that fear — not hatred — is the opposite of love and love's largest obstacle.

Blaming the Victim

It is difficult to accept responsibility for what we do wrong. Hence, we often see victimizers shifting the blame to those they have victimized. Blaming the victim is an illusion that we have no faults and must be better than those who are injured. We do not have to be victimizers to be under this illusion. In a patriarchal society, for example, men are raised in a culture treating women as inferior, so that men blame women for their own errors and wrongs.

---

[62] Tommy Rosa and Stephen Sinatra, MD, *Health Revelations from Heaven and Earth,* Rodale Inc., New York, 2015, page 57.

Authority

"In fourteen hundred ninety-two
Columbus sailed the ocean blue."

And after Columbus got to the Americas, there followed the subjugation of indigenous peoples, the slave trade, and the biggest land grab and seizure of natives' natural resources that the world has ever known. Portugal and Spain divided the new world between them, so that Portugal colonized Brazil and Spain laid claim to Mexico and the western coast of North America. Even ocean trade routes were divided between the two countries. The Americas, however, were not the only object of European greed and oppression; Africa, too, was divided into European colonies in which the original habitants lost their human rights.

What we abhor today was sanctioned in 1493 by Pope Alexander VI's papal bull, *Inter Caetera,* which proclaimed the right of Portugal and Spain to colonize the indigenous people of North and South America. It asserted that these countries had the right to convert and enslave those they conquered, and the enslavement of Africans was given the green light as well. The only exception was for land under the dominion of a Christian monarch (king or prince). This land give-away and right to enslave and convert was given to the kings of Castile and Leon "forever."

Later papal decrees condemned making slaves of non-Christians, and on February 15, 2017 Pope Francis publicly stated that indigenous people had the right to determine what happened to their land.

Much of this was skimmed over or totally omitted in my high school history classes, hidden under the praises of the European conquerors and the myth that the eventual domination of Native Americans was but a prelude to the "manifest destiny" of the United States expanding gloriously from coast to coast. In recent times many have become more aware of this travesty, leading some to fight to do away with Columbus Day.

It is obvious that the Spanish and Portuguese colonizers, along with those of other European nations as well, followed the letter of the law to cause irreparable harm to the native inhabitants of the Americas. Theirs is an example of the illusion of righteousness that comes from legalistic behavior. Nations can make some laws that turn legal acts into illegal acts and vice-versa, such as traffic or income tax laws. They have no right, however, to justify immoral behavior. If a country allows husbands to abuse their wives, we are obligated to condemn not only the husbands who practice such behavior, but also the nations that allow wives to be beaten.

The illusion of legalism — justifying one's behavior because it is legal — is one of the most deceptive illusions that impede one's practice of unconditional love. Blind acceptance of any authority leads one to believe that one is doing good by not breaking any laws. "I was doing what I was told" was not acceptable for the Nazi guards of concentration camps, nor is it ever acceptable.

Love, on the contrary, is far more than not doing wrong. This is the lesson Jesus gave to the rich man, who had not broken any of the commandments:

> Jesus looked at the man, and his heart went out to him, and he said, "There is still one thing wanting in you; go and sell all that you have, and give to the poor, and you will have wealth in heaven; then come and follow me." But the man's face clouded at these words, and he went away distressed, for he had great possessions. (Mark 10:21-22, OEB)

A second illusion of legalism is that we are better than others because we do not break any laws:

> Another time, speaking to people who were satisfied that they were religious, and who regarded everyone else with scorn, Jesus told this parable — "Two men went up into the Temple Courts to pray. One was a Pharisee and the other a tax-gatherer. The Pharisee stood forward and began praying to himself in this way — 'God, I thank you that I am not like other men — thieves, rogues, adulterers — or even like this tax-gatherer. I fast twice a week, and give a tenth of everything I get to God.' Meanwhile the tax-gatherer stood at a distance, not venturing even to raise his eyes to heaven, but he kept striking his breast and saying 'God, have mercy on me, a sinner.' This man, I tell you, went home pardoned, rather than the other. For everyone who exalts himself will be humbled, while everyone who humbles himself will be exalted." (Luke 18:9-14, OEB)

The Pharisee was self-satisfied, because he had kept all the laws. His illusion kept him from understanding that being loving is much more than not doing wrong.

A third illusion, implicit in the Scripture verse above, is that we think we can classify people into groups according to human norms. In other words, we are led into arbitrary practices of partiality:

> If you keep the royal law which runs — 'You must love your neighbor as you love yourself,' you are doing right; but, if you discriminate, you commit a sin, and stand convicted by that same law of being offenders against it. (James 2:8-9, OEB)

Partiality is fostered by the illusion that wealth, education, social status, culture, religion, or other human factors make one person better than another. We are mistakenly led to treating others as second-class citizens, like those who may have broken the law but have paid their debt to society. We let such distinctions guide us down the wrong path, away from the realization that we are all children of the same Father.

29

Belief Systems

Among the most feared natural disasters are earthquakes. Although we still cannot predict when they will occur, we now know what causes them. Huge sections of the earth's crust, called tectonic plates, slide slowly against each other. As they slide, the pressure builds. The release of pressure creates an earthquake.

The notion of tectonic plates is new in science. In 1910, F.B. Taylor theorized continental drift. Since he had little evidence, his proposal received minimal support. In 1915, Alfred Wegener, a German scientist, published *The Origin of Continents and Oceans.* He, too, proposed a theory of continental drift, suggesting that two hundred million years ago there was but one continent, Pangaea ("all land"), which gradually broke into smaller continents.

Unlike Taylor, Wegener built strong supporting arguments. He bolstered his radical thesis with fossil evidence, rock structures, prehistoric similarities in climate, and the way the eastern coastline of South America could fit into the western coastline of Africa. Science had already shown that areas now arid or tropical were once carved by glaciers. As a climatologist, Wegener thought it more sensible to postulate drifting continents than dramatic climate changes. His theory also solved the problem of how plants and animals could migrate over vast ocean expanses.

As soon as Wegener's book was translated into English, it encountered criticism and derision. The primary objection was the lack of a sufficient energy source to move huge land masses. Regardless, Wegener held to his theories until his death in 1930.

The coastline argument was discounted until the 1960s, when Sir Edward Bullard and two associates created a computerized map that fitted the continents together at a depth of nine hundred meters. The results were better than anyone had imagined possible.

In the years following Wegener's death, technological advances made possible extensive mapping of the ocean floor and created increased data on the earth's magnetic poles. These factors were crucial in testing Wegener's postulates. We learned that as iron-rich rocks form, they are magnetized in the direction of the earth's magnetic poles. An examination of these rocks, formed in different time periods, indicated polar wandering, that is, migration of the poles over time. (This could also be explained by continental drift.) Another discovery was that occasionally, perhaps due to sun spots, the earth's poles reverse their polarity, with the south becoming the north and the north becoming the south. New techniques in mapping the ocean floor showed mirror images of alternating strips of normal and reverse polarity on each side of the Pacific Ocean ridges. The theory of the ocean floor spreading and moving the continents apart was significantly bolstered.

In 1968 a new theory of plate tectonics was firmly supported in the scientific community. Previous hostility to Wegener's theories caved in to a new scientific model that not only supported continental drift, but was actually more extensive. That model is now used to explain earthquakes, and we take for granted that at the San Andreas Fault in California the North American plate is moving south and the Pacific plate is moving north.

Today the "experts" who ridiculed Wegener are not worth mention. Time has turned an arrogant majority opinion into an example of stubborn self-deception.

Scientific Worldviews

Civilization has held onto many world views throughout its known history. The Hebrews believed in a three-tiered universe, with the earth in the middle, the lower world of the dead and of demons below, and above a solid sky or firmament the realm of the divine. This was the world view of the Jews in Jesus's time.

During the Middle Ages the earth was thought to be the center of the universe, with the sun circling around it. In 1543 Nicholas Copernicus published a work stating that the earth goes around the sun while revolving on its axis. Galileo Galilei made improvements on the telescope and supported the theories of Copernicus. Like Wegener, Galileo met stubborn resistance, not from scientists, but from the Catholic Church, which said he was contradicting the Bible. He was placed under house arrest, and his book, *Dialogues,* was placed on the Index of

Forbidden Books, where it remained for over two hundred years.

Since Galileo, scientists changed their thinking to view the solar system as the universe, and then later it became evident that the solar system is part of a larger galaxy. Even that view changed, when astronomers realized that what they thought were stars were actually other galaxies; the earth is no longer the center of the universe, but an insignificant planet in an insignificant solar system in just another galaxy in an immeasurable universe.

Worldviews and Belief Systems

Every human being with the use of reason has a belief system or world view — or perhaps several world views of different kinds, such as scientific, religious, social, or political. Since we have to make sense of the world around us, we put the data together to make it fit into our perception of how everything works. Many of our views have been learned from our parents or others. Some of them have changed through education or personal experience. Sometimes we are forced to revise our belief system because we see apparent contradictions that must be reconciled.

Problems Caused by Belief Systems

Belief systems are a necessary part of our thought process; we cannot maneuver intelligently without them. At the same time they can clash, causing disputes, oppression and even war. College professors can lose tenure by proposing a theory outside commonly held views. Teachers can be forced to teach specific views for the religious or political reasons of those in authority. Physicians can be ostracized for promoting treatments outside the pharmaceutical model.

A belief system that holds that its tenets are true and that whatever contradicts it is false is called an *ideology*. The major premises of political parties usually constitute an ideology, and so do the personal beliefs people have about such things as diet and climate change. The most common belief systems, however, are those of most religions. Once a member, one can be under overwhelming social pressure to remain a member. If one leaves, excommunication can result, making the defector an outcast of one's former religious community. In early Christianity, the most egregious sin was apostasy, which always resulted in excommunication.

Whenever anyone fully adopts an ideology, there is a sense of security, because one is convinced of possessing the truth. Furthermore, ideologies tend to reinforce themselves, since those who buy into them will, most of the time, read, listen to, or take seriously only what they already agree with.

It should be clear why ideologies make dialog and compromise nearly impossible. When two groups of people get together to discuss their differing views, they may come away with a better understanding of an opposite position, but a conviction that "I am right and all who disagree are wrong" makes discussion useless.

Whenever anyone adheres to the belief that "I am right and you are wrong" on any topic, there is a concomitant belief in one's superiority over another. For example, members of various religions may join with each other and explicitly acknowledge that all are equal. That sounds good, but when they join in their own houses of worship, they profess what they really believe: "I have the true belief. My form of worship is the correct one. My rituals are better than others. My community is better than others." Although various religions will adamantly profess that all religious professions deserve to be treated equally, that does not mean an acceptance of true equality for everyone, but only that we should act *as though* all are equal. In other words, we make religious equality a legal fiction, a game of "Let's pretend."

One of the buzz words for our time is tolerance. We are supposed to be tolerant of those whose beliefs, rituals, customs, race, or gender is different than our own. Tolerance, however, is not the same as acceptance — acceptance of others as actual equals. Ideologies, including religious belief systems, may preach tolerance, but may at the same time implicitly (or even explicitly) proclaim superiority of both their doctrines and their adherents over all who are different.

The Extreme Belief System

Belief systems can usually be put into categories on the basis of which dogmas are accepted and what kind of dogmas are believed. There are religious and political belief systems, and among religious systems we find diverse religions, such as Jewish, Muslim, and Christian. And Christian religions can be further divided into Protestant, Catholic, Orthodox and others. In the miscellaneous category there is the belief system of those who simply hold that their opinion — on whatever subject — is the only correct one. The certitude that "I am right and you are wrong" is an easy illusion to fall into.

From the time we reach the use of reason we are constantly ranked according to our intelligence. Report cards, gold stars, and honor roll certificates separate the smarter kids from the dumber kids. Those who excel receive scholarships that put them in the select class of those with college degrees. Graduates are further separated into those who are "summa cum laude," "magna cum laude," "4.0" and so on. To a large extent — although with many exceptions — those with the highest rankings go on to get the positions with the most political and economic power.

The more one esteems one's intelligence, the greater can be the illusion of being better than other people — greater than those who are not quite as bright.

If we are blessed with a high degree of intelligence, we need to be grateful, but without feeling superior because of it. If you have a position of authority or employment with a high income, be wary of the illusion that you deserve this because you are smarter or better than others.

A highly educated person may have the illusion that her/his opinions are better than those of others. This illusion becomes extreme in those with extreme power. There are cases in which some are so attached to their opinion that they will twist facts to prove their point, such as concerning climate change, the effects of tobacco on health, abortion, birth control, divorce and remarriage, and labor unions. At times advocates of one side or the other have presented false reports; white papers have been written using only carefully chosen data; leaders in government have asked their intelligence agencies to come up with the results they desire. And then there are those who scour the Scriptures to find the exact verses to prove their doctrine, while ignoring whatever contradicts it.

So convinced in their own opinions are some, that they would compel others to follow their moral restrictions. Whenever the occasion arises to say, "I am right and you are wrong," it is time to step back and question whether we are truly intellectually superior and whether we truly believe that others are our equals. The illusion of intellectual superiority leads to imagining superiority in many other ways and makes us forget we are all God's children.

Dialogue

A frequently proposed solution to enable disputing parties to reach agreement and/or act together is dialogue. With the hope that divisions can be healed by reaching common points of agreement, we accept the notion that honest discussion can replace hostility and violence.

This approach cannot succeed if either party holds to being right while any opposition is wrong. When parties come to the table convinced of their infallibility, dialogue is impossible.

Healing Division

The root cause of divisions is a divisive way of thinking, which in turn is perpetuated by ideologies proclaiming that they alone offer what is true and morally upright. In this, the belief systems of organized religions, including Christianity, are not exempt. It is not enough to act *as though* others are equal to us, while at the same time internally believing that others are inferior because they lack true doctrine, true morality, or true rituals and form of worship. We must change our way of thinking so that we actually accept others as true equals, instead of tolerating them as inferior because they do not have our belief system and culture.

To change our way of thinking is difficult. Ideologies, along with all their adherents, never want to admit ever being wrong. One of our most difficult psychological tasks is to apologize. Witness the frequent false apologies that begin with the phrase, "If anyone is offended..."

Somewhere and somehow, we have to begin. It is only by reforming our belief system into one in which we truly believe that we are all truly equal in value and dignity before God, that we can begin to understand a different point of view, and it is only by seeing others through their eyes that we can begin an honest dialog on those issues on which we disagree.

To heal divisions we must treat the cause of our illness and not just the symptoms. We need to reform our ideologies, if not abandon them altogether. We must change our way of thinking to one in which we do not just tolerate others, but accept them as true equals.

Light of the World

Jesus again addressed the people. "I am the light of the world," he said. "The person who follows me will not walk in darkness, but will have the light of life." (John 8:12 OEB)

It is you who are the light of the world. A town that stands on a hill cannot be hidden. People do not light a lamp and put it under a basket, but on the lamp-stand, where it gives light to everyone in the house. Let your light so shine before the eyes of others so that, seeing your good actions, they will praise your Father who is in heaven. (Matthew 5:14-16 OEB)

Christ is the light, light of the world, a light for all to see,
but know he calls you light as well, a light the same as he.

Though you may live without the sun, where joy of dawn
    ne'er rises,
though naught you see but shadows dim, with gloom that
    mesmerizes,

you need not seek to see the light in some far distant star;
enlightenment is found in you, in who and what you are.

For you are light, too bright to hide beneath a box or jar;
like fireworks atop a hill, all see from near and far.

Be unlike a candle flame, which breath can turn to smoke,
but like the sun, whose heat and light tsunami winds can't
    choke.

So many need the light you are. Know clearly what it's for.
Use your light of gold to lighten burdens of the poor.

Shine em'rald green of life on those who've lost the will to
    live.
Use celestial blue for those who struggle to forgive.

If another's life seems drab, use light of rosy red;
A silver ray for those whose lives to worldliness are wed.

Cast a royal purple cloak on those who are rejected.
Pour water crystal clear for those whose thirst has been
    neglected.

Reflect on this: you're not alone in glowing with your light;
the light of others blends with yours to make the whole
    world bright.

With others you are stars at night, that twinkle with a spark
of laughter just like fireflies that sparkle in the dark.

So dance with glee like lightning bugs that little children
    chase,
and draw a smile from ear to ear on every small child's
    face.

Your light's not made from straw or coal; no matches do
    you need.
Electric power is useless, and your flames no fuel can feed.

Your light is not created by your deeds or what you do.
Your works are more like windows that your light comes
    shining through.

The light you share is light of God, in multicolored hues.
The more you share, the more you have, brilliant and
    profuse.

To see your light will serve for all to gratefully extol
the Source of rainbows filtered through the prism of your
    soul.

Part VIII

The Challenge of

Unconditional Love

30

Our Purpose in Life

Children learn better when they are not hungry during school hours. Some families lack the income to provide breakfast or lunch money for their children. What will be the benefits to a child in these circumstances to have breakfast and lunch provided? Will it change the probability of that child graduating from high school? Or of becoming a productive member of society?

Everything you do for another — just giving a cup of cold water to a child — will be rewarded.

> And, if anyone gives but a cup of cold water to one of these little ones because they are a disciple, I tell you that they will assuredly not lose their reward." (Matthew 10:42, OEB) [63]

---

[63] See also Mark 9:41.

Your good deeds may help someone else, but they may also help many others, and even you. Everything has consequences, most of which are unseen.

The consequences of our actions can be deceptive. We are under the illusion that we are all separate and disconnected. This misconception distorts our perception of the consequences of our actions. We think that by smoking no one is harmed but ourselves. Or we imagine that by short-changing a customer only that person is injured and that we have profited. The consequences of our acts are all interconnected, just as everything in the universe is one.

A second illusion is that small acts of kindness have little impact on global problems, and that only major attacks on oppressors are the only acts of consequence. It was stated earlier that we must always take whatever steps are necessary and possible to protect the innocent, the use of force permissible only as a defense against injury. Love, however, is ultimately the only effective weapon against evil.

We are not able to overcome all evils in the world, no matter how many we persuade to join us. God does not expect that of us. But we are responsible for ourselves — how we act and react in our own limited world and in our finite allotted time. Do not underestimate what loving acts can achieve, for they channel the love and power of our Father.

We all have a purpose for our life: to grow in unconditional love, which is to become more godlike:

God is love; and whoever lives in love lives in God, and God lives in them. (1 John 4:16, OEB)

"You, then, must become perfect — as your heavenly Father is perfect." (Matthew 5:48, OEB)

You do not have to look far and wide for the resources to reach your goal, for they are already within you. Look for the God within. You are a child of God; you have always been a child of God; and you will always be a child of God. God's love lives in you.

31

Thy Kingdom Come

Contrary to the illusion of our separate existence in this life is the perception that all of humanity, the entire earth, and even all in the universe are interrelated and exist in unity. If so, then our most insignificant actions and most secret thoughts have effects that rebound throughout all that is. We are like cells in the body of humankind. When one cell is sick, the whole body is sick. When one cell grows spiritually, the whole body is blessed.

Every one of us has a purpose in life that goes beyond oneself. Love is not true love if it is concerned only with oneself, while neglecting the world in which one lives. By changing ourselves, we change our world at the same time.

Jesus commanded us to change our lives and our way of thinking, while in the context of looking forward to the coming kingdom of God. Even though his expectations of a cataclysmic, divine intervention to usher in the kingdom within the lifetime of his hearers failed to come to pass, we still pray, "Thy kingdom come." It is still our goal to prepare for God's kingdom, for a society in which "Thy will be done, on earth as it is in heaven."

We are called to make society better, not just by eliminating injustice, but by converting it into a world that positively expresses God's love. The following are some of the changes to look for in a world that has become the kingdom of God:

- Instead of respecting those in authority because of their position, we will bestow authority on those who have earned our respect.
- Civil laws will not be manipulated into loopholes to excuse selfishness, but be true instruments to correct injustices and point adherents toward ethical behavior.
- Rather than those who have much while acquiring even more, the wealthy will express empathy by sharing and enabling those who lack the necessities of life to benefit equally from the world's resources.
- The suffering who are out of sight will not be out of mind, but the object of the blessings of those both near and far.
- The disabled will have the means to share their gifts and talents with others.
- Those who are different in any way will be treasured for their unique contributions to society.
- We will restore to the earth what we consume, with respect for nature and for all living beings.

- We will treat others as equals because we truly believe that others are our sisters and brothers with the same Father.
- The primary, universal religious ritual will be unconditional love for all.

The goal of practicing unconditional love does not imply giving up living life to the fullest. Helping others to enjoy life makes one's own life more enjoyable. To be sure, accomplishing this purpose in life may at times be difficult, and at times appear impossible. But we must begin, and we must persevere, for the roadblocks that seem unconquerable are an illusion.

We are not powerless. In a spirit of *giving thanks*, we *perceive* our true nature as God's children, one family, with the divine powers of *forgiving*, *blessing*, and *praying*. We need but to *express our love by our actions*.

> But Jesus said again, "My children, how hard a thing it is to enter the kingdom of God! It is easier for a camel to get through a needle's eye, than for a rich person to enter the kingdom of God."
>
> "Then who can be saved?" they exclaimed in the greatest astonishment. Jesus looked at them, and answered, "With people it is impossible, but not with God; for everything is possible with God."[64]

---

[64] Mark 10:24-27, OEB.

Stay Awake — A Meditation

Presently they came to a garden known as Gethsemane, and Jesus said to his disciples "Sit down here while I pray." He took with him Peter, James, and John; and began to show signs of great dismay and deep distress of mind. "I am sad at heart," he said, "sad even to death; wait here, and watch." Going on a little further, he threw himself on the ground, and began to pray that, if it were possible, he might be spared that hour. "Abba, Father," he said, "all things are possible to you; take away this cup from me; yet, not what I will, but what you will.

Then he came and found the three apostles asleep. "Simon," he said to Peter, "are you asleep? Couldn't you watch for one hour? Watch and pray," he said to them all, "so that you may not fall into temptation. True, the spirit is willing, but the flesh is weak." Again he went away, and prayed in the same words; and coming back again he found them asleep, for their eyes were heavy; and they did not know what to say to him.

> A third time he came, and said to them, "Sleep on
> now, and rest yourselves. Enough! My time has
> come. Look, the Son of Man is being betrayed
> into the hands of wicked people. Up, and let us
> be going. Look! My betrayer is close at hand."
> (Mark 14:32-42 OEB)

It's time to rest, refresh your soul; it's time to turn within.
So, close your eyes, relax yourself, away from noise and din.
Go deep within, within yourself — go deeper, deeper still.
Greet those along your path within. Toward all you feel
     goodwill.

As slowly down the path you walk, look deep within your
     soul.
You'll see a garden growing there, on grassy, verdant knoll.
Roses, tulips, daffodils — all flowers are in bloom.
The whistle of a gentle breeze is filled with their perfume.

A winding path you follow till the central place you find,
and there within the garden's center is a tree enshrined.
This tree majestic towers tall, its branches fill the sky.
Its fruit is ripe, and soft, and sweet, and tempting to the eye.

To take one bite will lead to two, and then to three and four.
It matters not how much you eat, you always will want more.
This is the fruit of love of wealth, of pleasure, power, and
     greed.
Take a little, want a lot, consume more than you need.

Eat from this tree and you will know both good and bad
     firsthand.
The urge to eat and eat some more, you simply can't with-
     stand.
For this tree's fruit, like alcohol, or drugs, or nicotine

will coat your eyes with fog and smoke, make other fruit un-
      seen.

If only from this tree you eat, you slowly will be lulled
into a dreary, dreamless sleep, with all your senses dulled.
Then like a zombie, living dead, you'll sleepwalk in the
      night,
and only eat to feed your sleep, and hide the real from sight.

Now look beyond this tree and see a lonely figure there.
Look closely, feel his agony, and listen to his prayer:
"Abba, were it possible, then take this cup from me,
yet not my will but yours be done — be done as you decree."

Behold the man who throws himself upon the ground to
      pray.
Look into his eyes and hear him plead with you and say,
"Stay with me and pray with me. Just stay with me one hour.
Pray the darkness of this night will not your strength de-
      vour."

"I beg you, stay here, watch with me — yes, watch and keep
      awake.
Share my grief and agony; my heart's about to break.
Are you asleep? Don't fall asleep! No, do not close your
      eyes.
A willing spirit trapped in flesh must from its weakness
      rise."

Your eyes are weighted down with sleep, your body numb-
      ness feels.
The fruit you've eaten clouds your mind; with sleep your
      body reels.
But as you fight to stay awake, to watch one hour with him,
your ears begin to hear again, your eyes become less dim.

And as you focus on his face, your garden scene comes clear.
Another tree climbs to the sky; its branches now appear.
No sugar high will its fruit cause; instead it satisfies.
This is the tree of life divine, true wisdom in disguise.

This fruit is love for far and near, for enemies and friends;
it's to be sorry for your crimes, and then to make amends.
It's living the beatitudes, forgiveness with a smile.
It's giving more than asked of you — to walk the extra mile.

To seek God's kingdom first is what this tree will ask of you:
to live for life that never dies — eternal life pursue.
Pluck the fruit from this tree's branches; it will you illumi-
        nate.
Choose the path of life it offers: it will set your thinking
        straight.

Look closely now into the face of one who soon will die.
Stay awake and watch with him whose death is drawing
        nigh.
His will to choose the tree of life presents a mystery:
by choosing tree of life, you see, he chose to die upon a tree.

Now it is your time to choose: the tree where knowledge
        stultifies,
or tree where life and love preside and Spirit sanctifies.
Your meditation's over now. You've learned how to deci-
        sions make.
When I count down, your eyes will open. Three, two, one —
        now wide awake!

References

Braden, Gregg, *The Isaiah Effect, Decoding the Lost Science of Prayer and Prophecy*, New York: Harmony Books, 2000, pages 145-181.

Didache, Chapters 10:6, 16:7-8. This is a short Christian document which may have been written as early as the end of the first century. An English translation can be found in the following: Bart D. Ehrman,, *Lost Scriptures, Books that Did Not Make It into the New Testament*, New York: Oxford University Press, 2003, pages 211-217. The *Didache* is also on the Internet online.

Dossey, Larry, M.D., *Healing Words: The Power of Prayer and the Practice of Medicine,* HarperSanFrancisco, 1993, page 79, 97.

Holy Bible From the Ancient Eastern Text, George M. Lamsa's Translations From the Aramaic of the Peshitta, HarperSanFrancisco, 1968.

Jeremias, Joachim, *Jerusalem in the Time of Jesus,* Philadelphia: Fortress Press, 1975, pp. 320-354.

The Jerusalem Bible, Doubleday & Company, New York: Garden City, 1966.

Ritchie, George G., with Elizabeth Sherrill, *Return from Tomorrow,* Old Tappan, New Jersey: Fleming H. Revell Company, 1978, page 116. This book gives an amazing account of Ritchie's near-death experience in 1943, and the events following are equally interesting. The author is one of the primary influences in Dr. Raymond Moody's exploration of near-death experiences.

Rosa, Tommy and Stephen Sinatra, MD, *Health Revelations from Heaven and Earth,* New York: Rodale Inc., 2015, pages 36, 57.

Suggested Reading

Bibles

Holy Bible. I suggest using several versions at the same time. The New Revised Standard Version is an excellent translation, but every version, including the NRSV, has both advantages and drawbacks. I also recommend using a comprehensive concordance, which will give the original Hebrew and Greek words for all English words, along with the meaning of the source words at the time they were written. Usually a concordance uses the English words found in the original King James Version.

Scripture

Bultman, Rudolf, *The History of the Synoptic Tradition.* This is an excellent source for information on the historical development of Mark, Matthew and Luke.

Jeremias, Joachim, *The Lord's Prayer*. This is a small pamphlet of only thirty-nine pages, but it gives a clear and thorough explanation of the Lord's Prayer as it would have been understood in the first century.

Jeremias, Joachim, *The Parables of Jesus*. Jeremias analyzes the parables in their historical and biblical context. References are extensive.

DeWall, Clement, *False Questions: Jesus and Our Spiritual Path*. This book provides an explanation of various misinterpreted parts of the Gospels and of historical religious events.

Ehrman, Bart D., *Jesus, Interrupted, Revealing the Hidden Contradictions in the Bible (and Why We Don't Know About Them)*. This is a good historical account of the development of the New Testament and early Christianity.

Ehrman, Bart D., *Misquoting Jesus, The Story Behind Who Changed the Bible and Why*. Ehrman tells the story of the scribes who copied biblical manuscripts.

Helms, Randel McCraw, *Who Wrote The Gospels*. The author uses internal evidence (information found in the Gospels) to ascertain the background of the evangelists and how the Gospels were written.

Pagels, Elaine, *The Gnostic Gospels*. Of special interest is the author's explanation of how politics played a role in forming Christian doctrine.

Pagels, Elaine, *Revelations, Visions, Prophecy, & Politics in the Book of Revelation*. The work covers the book of Revelation and puts it into a clearly understood historical setting.

Religious History

Eusebius' Ecclesiastical History, Complete and Unabridged — New Updated Edition. The version of Church history written by Eusebius provided the framework for historians for centuries. It is invaluable in giving us quotations from other works no longer extant.

The New Complete Works of Josephus, translated by William Whiston, Commentary by Paul L. Maier. Josephus was a Jewish historian who lived shortly after the time of Jesus. He avoided anything that would offend the Romans who supported him after the destruction of Jerusalem, but he recorded historical details not found elsewhere.

Life after Death

Atwater, P.M.H., *Beyond the Light, The Mysteries and Revelations of Near-Death Experiences.* The author goes into both negative and positive near-death experiences and discusses their aftereffects in depth. She also explores the physical or biological side of the experience.

Atwater, P.M.H., *The Big Book of Near-Death Experiences: The Ultimate Guide to What Happens When We Die.* Atwater is both a near-death experience and a consummate researcher. This book is an encyclopedia of near-death experiences and their after-effects.

Atwater, P.M.H., *Coming Back to Life, The After-Effects of The Near-Death Experience.* Atwater is one of the rare researchers who has actually experienced an NDE. Her book is not only for those who have had a personal NDE, but for those who have been close to death in other ways. It covers the transformation of both individuals and humanity as a whole.

Atwater, P.M.H., LH.D., *The New Children and Near-Death Experiences.* Atwater studies children who have had NDEs and how they have changed.

Bowman, Carol, *Children's Past Lives, How Past Life Memories Affect Your Child.* The author relates stories, including her own, about children who remember past lives and how remembering helped them. The last half of the book is devoted to helping parents deal with their children and discern true past lives.

Bowman, Carol, *Return from Heaven, Beloved Relatives Reincarnated Within Your Family.* Here are stories of relatives reincarnated into the same family.

Brinkley, Dannion, *At Peace in the Light.* Brinkley fills in details of his life and personal experience. He further discusses how to help those who are dying and describes the types of centers he is dedicated to building.

Brinkley, Dannion, *Saved by the Light, The True Story of a Man Who Died Twice and the Profound Revelations He Received.* The author gives a vivid account of his near-death experience. One of the most remarkable facets of his story is the total change in character that he underwent as a result of his NDE.

Currie, Ian, *You Cannot Die, Spiritual Accounts of Life Before Life.* Because of its thoroughness, this book has much to offer many years after its initial publication in 1978. The author covers nearly every aspect of life after death.

Eadie, Betty J., *The Awakening Heart, My continuous journey to love.* We learn how the author's life changed after her NDE. She tells of her experience with her children before being born and how they decided before birth to stay together in this life. She explains how her first marriage fell apart and how her religious attitudes changed. She believes we should not impose our religious beliefs on others.

Eadie, Betty J., *Embraced by the Light.* This is one of the most complete NDEs found in NDE literature. She gives principles concerning prayer, and for her Satan is a reality.

Fenimore, Angie, *Beyond the Darkness, My Near-Death Journey to the Edge of Hell and Back.* This is a brief autobiography of a woman who attempted suicide and returned to tell her story. Her experience is preceded by numerous stories of other negative experiences, but her NDE is intriguing and makes the book worthwhile.

Gallup, George, Jr., *Adventures in Immortality.* This book gives statistics and commentary on a survey begun in 1980 and ending in September 1981.

Grey, Margot, *Return from Death, An Explanation of the Near-Death Experience.* The author describes an intense NDE in February 1976.

Guggenheim, Bill, and Judy Guggenheim, *Hello From Heaven! A new field of research — After-Death Communications — confirms that life and love are eternal.* The authors give an extremely wide variety of accounts in which one or more persons experience some kind of communication with a deceased person. Although the book enters a relatively new field of study, its breadth of experiences offers much that would serve as the basis for a sociological study. Their cases, if taken seriously, have far-reaching theological consequences.

Hinze, Sarah, *Coming from the Light, Spiritual Accounts of Life Before Life.* Sarah Hinze broke new ground by offering many accounts of children who chose their parents before coming to earth. The book gives parents a deeper appreciation of their children, and it gives everyone a new way of thinking about one's purpose in life.

Martin, Joel, and Patricia Romanowski, *Love Beyond Life, The Healing Power of After-Death Communications.* This is a collection of various after-death or spirit communications. The stories confirm what the Guggenheims relate, but there is more discussion and analysis in this book. It might have been better to have let the stories speak for themselves.

Martin, Joel, and Patricia Romanowski, *Our Children Forever, George Anderson's Messages from Children on the Other Side.* A primary thesis of the book is that children who die remain close to their parents and loved ones. There is much to comfort and console parents who have lost a child, and the details are convincing.

Moody, Raymond, Ph.D., *Glimpses of Eternity, Sharing a Loved One's Passage from This Life to the Next.* Dr. Moody relates multiple accounts of people sharing the same visions of loved ones passing from this life to the next. These accounts refute the debunkers' claims of hallucinations, drugs, and medications as the cause of these experiences.

Moody, Raymond A., Jr., M.D., *Life After Life.* This is one of Moody's first works, giving cases of near-death experiences.

Moody, Raymond A., Jr., M.D., *Reunions, Visionary Encounters with Departed Loved Ones.* Dr. Moody has created a place with special rooms, mirror, and furnishings, along with techniques for contacting the dead. The book relates some of his clients' personal experiences.

Moody, Raymond A., Jr., M.D., *The Light Beyond, New Explorations.* Moody relates the typical NDE and explains some of the changes in one's life afterward.

Moody, Raymond, M.D., *Reunions, Visionary Encounters with Departed Loved Ones.* Dr. Moody relates experiences of persons in controlled surroundings and their encounters with departed loved ones.

Morse, Melvin, M.D., *Closer to the Light, Learning from the Near-Death Experiences of Children.* Morse demonstrates that the numerous cases of children's NDEs must be taken seriously. He asserts that these cases have no scientific explanation. The children have perceptions of details they should not be able to know, and they are personally transformed.

Morse, Melvin, M.D., *Transformed by the Light, The Powerful Effect of Near-Death Experiences on People's Lives.* This is a compilation of people's near-death experiences and how their lives were changed.

Rawlings, Maurice, M.D., *Beyond Death's Door.* This is one of the few books to discuss negative NDEs.

Ring, Kenneth, Ph.D., *Heading Toward Omega, In Search of the Meaning of the Near-Death Experience*. This book is intended to awaken us to the evolutionary implication of NDEs.

Ring, Kenneth, Ph.D., *Life at Death, A Scientific Investigation of the Near-Death Experience*. Ring is a sociologist who writes with these purposes in mind: (1) To know how frequent the experience is. (2) To see whether illness, accident, or suicide makes a difference in the experience. (3) To find the relationship between religiousness and the core experience. (4) To determine how lives are changed by NDEs. This is one of the few well documented sociological studies of NDEs.

Ritchie, George G., M.D., *My Life After Dying, Becoming Alive to Universal Love*. This is Ritchie's second book. Here he gives more of his personal opinions about life.

Schwartz, Gary E., Ph.D., *The Afterlife Experiments, Breakthrough Scientific Evidence of Life After Death*. Professional, recognized mediums are put through double-blind tests to ascertain their accuracy.

Southerland, Cherie, Ph.D., *Reborn in the Light, Life After Near-Death Experiences*. This is an important sociological work about the effects of NDEs. It complements and confirms the research of Kenneth Ring, and has added significance because the author's work was done outside the US (in Australia).

Steiger, Brad, and Sherry Hansen Steiger, *Children of the Light, The Startling and Inspiring Truth about Children's Near-Death Experiences and How The Illumine the Beyond*. This work is a collection of children's near-death experiences. Not all of them were told to the authors directly. Some are indicative of reincarnation.

Stevenson, Ian, M.D., *Twenty Cases Suggestive of Reincarnation*, Second Edition, Revised and Enlarged. Although there have been many books on reincarnation in recent times, this book is a ground-breaking classic. Stevenson concentrates on children and never uses hypnosis. The accounts are thorough and detailed.

Weiss, Brian, M.D., *Many Lives, Many Masters*. Weiss tells how he fell into past-life regression therapy in a way that changed his life and the lives of his patients.

Weiss, Brian, M.D., *Messages from the Masters, Tapping into the Power of Love*. The author relates stories from his past-life regression therapy sessions, with the theme of the power of love. He includes exercises and meditations.

Whitton, Joel L., M.D., Ph.D., and Joe Fisher, *Life Between Life, Scientific Explorations into the Void Separating One Incarnation from the Next.* This work gives numerous cases of persons under hypnosis and their reported experiences of living between their lives on earth.

Wooolgers, Roger J., Ph.D., *Other Lives, Other Selves; A Jungian Psychotherapist Discovers Past Lives.* This is a hypnotherapist's view on reincarnation and past lives.

Printed in Great
Britain
by Amazon